IN AND OUT OF PARADISE

*The Book of Genesis
from Adam and Eve
to the Tower of Babel*

Conrad E. L'Heureux

PAULIST PRESS
New York/Ramsey

Copyright © 1983 by
Conrad E. L'Heureux

Library of Congress
Catalog Card Number: 82-62415

ISBN: 0-8091-2530-7

Published by Paulist Press
545 Island Road, Ramsey, N.J. 07446

Printed and bound in the
United States of America

Contents

To
Gerard and Jeannette

Preface

This book grew out of my undergraduate teaching at the University of Dayton. I was continually confronted by the question, "How does a reasonable person living in the twentieth century make sense out of such a far-fetched and apparently irrelevant story as the biblical account of Adam and Eve?" I knew that in order to help my students with questions such as this, I had to help them become familiar with the methods used by modern scholarship in studying the Bible. They also needed to be familiar with analogous literary materials composed in ancient times and rediscovered by archaeology. Finally, they had to be willing to go beyond the more objective and historical kinds of data in order to relate the story to their own experience. The five chapters of this book contain what I have arrived at, after considerable trial and error, as my way of answering the questions which my students ask. I sincerely hope that it will also prove helpful to a broader reading public.

I wish to thank the students at the University of Dayton who read the various versions the manuscript has been through and provided invaluable feedback. I am also grateful to my colleagues in the Department of Religious Studies who have given me their reactions in both formal and informal settings. A final word of thanks goes to my fellow-parishioners at St. Agnes Church in Dayton who provided the opportunity for testing this material in the context of adult education classes.

Chapter One

Genesis 1-11: The Text

We are all familiar with the distortions which arise when something is taken out of its context. It can be especially annoying when something we said is quoted back to us in such a way as to miss completely what we meant. It is also well known that this process of quoting out of context is one of the ways the Bible can be misused. So no one will disagree if we say that to interpret a biblical story, it must be understood within its proper context. It should be noted, however, that the word "context" here can be understood in narrower or broader terms. For example, we may say that a short phrase or clause is not understood unless it is seen in the context of the sentence of which it is a part. We may go further, however, and say that a given sentence must be seen in the context of the paragraph it comes from: the paragraph in the context of a chapter, the chapter in the context of the book, etc. In other words, context keeps broadening out into larger and larger concentric circles.

The passage which this book is most directly concerned with is the story of Adam and Eve in Genesis 2 and 3. There are, however, a number of ever broadening contexts in which this passage must be placed if we are to understand it properly. First, it must be understood as part of the story of the world before the time of Abraham, a story contained in Genesis 1-11 and which biblical scholars conventionally refer to as the Primeval History. We shall see shortly that some of the material in the

Primeval History, specifically the Adam and Eve story, was originally part of a literary work we call the *J* work. This *J* work, then, must be taken into consideration as one of the "broader" contexts of the story which interests us. The *J* work, in turn, can be seen in connection with two even broader contexts. The first is the context of ancient Near Eastern mythology, upon which the *J* author drew for some of the building blocks of his story. We will give special attention to this aspect in Chapter Two. The second of the broader contexts is the end result of the literary tradition of ancient Israel, namely the Bible itself. Though we will not devote as much attention to this aspect, we must at least recognize that some of the meanings of the story emerge only when it is seen in the context of later religious developments which produced the completed Bible and the two religious groups which claim it as their scripture: Christianity and Judaism.

The *J* Work

It was mentioned above that the Adam and Eve story was originally part of something called the *J* work. In this section, we will take a look at what that means.

Modern scholarship has long recognized that the material in the Primeval History is not the uniform, consistent account which one would expect if it were the work of a single author. That is to say, it is a *composite* work, put together from the work of more than one author. This observation was clearly stated in a book published in 1678 by the French Catholic priest, Richard Simon. While Simon could reach the negative conclusion that this was not the work of one author, he did not take any positive steps toward discovering just how the multiple authorship was to be analyzed in further detail. The decisive step was taken by another French Catholic scholar named Jean Astruc. In a work published in 1753, Astruc observed that some passages of the Primeval History consistently used the word Elohim (*'ĕlōhîm*) to refer to God. This is a general word which can be used as a common noun, like its English equivalent, to refer to the "God" of the Bible, as well as to "pagan gods." Other passages, on the other hand, prefer to call God Yahweh.[1] Yahweh is the name which ancient Israel used as the proper name of its God. That is, this word is never used for any other "god."

Some readers of the Bible might say that they have never seen this name Yahweh and so they will be surprised to hear that it is the special name of God in the Old Testament. Here is what happened. In the centuries immediately preceeding the time of Jesus, the Jewish community came to believe that the name Yahweh was so sacred that it should not be pronounced. When they came to this word in their Bibles, they did not pronounce it but instead said "Adonai," which means "Lord." Most English translations have followed this pious Jewish practice and print the word LORD instead of Yahweh. Here the O-R-D are in small capital letters in order to distinguish the cases where LORD represents the occurrence of Yahweh in the original Hebrew text from ordinary uses of the common noun "lord." The reader may want to check chapter 2 of Genesis in his or her Bible to see multiple examples of this LORD standing for Hebrew Yahweh. (The Jerusalem Bible, however, forms an exception to what was said in this paragraph, for it has broken with tradition and printed Yahweh instead of LORD.)

With the clue supplied by Astruc, it becomes possible to divide much of the material of the Primeval History into two blocks: the Elohim material and the Yahweh material. Once this is done, we can examine each of the two blocks and draw up a list of characteristic features for each type of material. This list then provides the criteria for assigning passages where God is not mentioned and where, therefore, the Elohim/Yahweh distinction does not help us determine to which of the two categories that text belongs.

If, at this stage, we were to carry the analysis *beyond* Genesis 11, we would continue to find material which was similar to the Elohim passages of Genesis 1-11. Since this material shows a strong interest in questions of worship, it has been called the Priestly source, or just *P*. Scholars believe it was written in the century following the destruction of Jerusalem in 587 B.C. On the other hand, the passages which are similar to the Yahweh texts of Genesis 1-11 are labeled *J* because the name is spelled "Jahweh" in German, the language of the scholars who first established the practice of using these abbreviations. The *J* work was probably written during the reign of Solomon (between 960 and 920 B.C.) on the basis of older material which had been handed on previously in oral tradition.

The seach for *J* and *P* material would take us through the books of Genesis, Exodus, Leviticus, Numbers and Deuteronomy. Those books make up the Pentateuch or Torah. Beginning with Genesis 15, however, our analysis would be complicated by discovery of a third type of material, that which scholars have labeled *E* for Elohist. This source stems from the northern Kingdom of Israel and is about a century later than the *J* work. *E* shares with *P* the preference for the divine name Elohim. There are, however, other significant differences between *E* and *P* which make it relatively easy to distinguish them. A fourth and last category is the *D* material. Some scholars think this is found only in the book of Deuteronomy, though others believe that there are some short *D* passages in the earlier books. In any case, the core of *D* was written in the seventh century B.C.

In summary, the first five books of the Bible appear to be a composite of what were originally four separate literary works (sources, or documents) labeled *J, E, D* and *P*, which were combined by editors to produce the text which we now have. The first stage of this process was the combination of *J* and *E*, which took place before the destruction of Jerusalem. Later, the combined *JE* was joined with *P*. Finally, Deuteronomy was inserted. These developments are summarized in the chart on page 7.

Though it is only a theory which cannot be proved conclusively, the "Documentary Hypothesis" outlined in the chart below seems to provide the most satisfactory explanation of the evidence and is accepted by the great majority of modern scholars. The methodology which allows us to separate the various sources is called "literary criticism" and was refined in the late nineteenth century by Julius Wellhausen.[2]

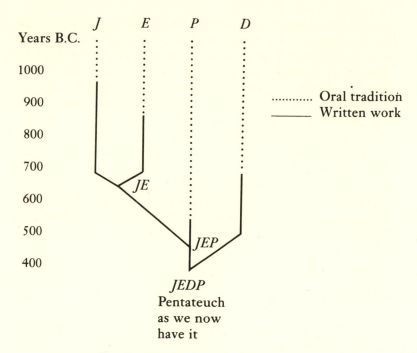

Chart 1: Formation of the Pentateuch

The *P* Creation Story

Perhaps the reader will, by this point, have had enough of theory. We will go on to look at the texts and see how the theory works out in practice. What follows will by no means constitute a definitive proof that the *JEDP* theory is correct. It will, however, illustrate how scholarship goes about its task and at least show that by dividing the Primeval History into its *J* and *P* components, we are able to make good sense out of otherwise puzzling phenomena.

The *P* creation story begins in Gen 1:1 and ends with Gen 2:4a. (The latter reference is to the first half of verse 4 in chapter 2.) A quick check will demonstrate that all modern translations

agree that a division must be made right in the middle of verse
4.³ It would be a good idea, at this point, to read Gen 1:1-2:4a
very carefully and then to keep the text handy for reference in
connection with the following summary of some of the important *P* characteristics which are found in this passage.

First of all, it will be noticed that the (translated) text speaks
of God rather than Yahweh or LORD. This reflects the fact that
the original Hebrew text has Elohim, one of the indicators of *P*
which has already been discussed. There are, however, other
less obvious but nonetheless clearly defined stylistic features in
the passage. One of the most striking is the repetitive and for-
mulaic nature of the account which emerges from a comparison
of the passages dealing with the first three days of creation.

Gen 1:3-5—First Day

3 God said, "Let there be light," and there was light.
4 God saw that the light was good and he divided the
   light from the darkness.
5 God called the light "day," and the darkness he called
   "night." It was evening, and then morning—the first
   day.

Gen 1:6-8—Second Day

6 Then God said, "Let there be a firmament between the
   waters, and let it divide the waters on the one hand
   from the waters on the other."
7 God made the firmament and he divided the waters
   above the firmament from the waters below the
   firmament, and it was so.
8 God called the firmament "sky." It was evening, and
   then morning—the second day.

Gen 1:9-10,13—Third Day

9 God said, "Let the waters below the sky be gathered
   into one place and let the dry land appear." And it was
   so.
10 God called the dry land "earth," and the gathered

13 waters he called "seas." God saw that it was good. . . .
It was evening, and then morning—the third day.

It will be seen that the creative activity of each day is stated according to a pattern, or formula which can be outlined as follows:

> God said, "Let there be. . . .
> And it was so.
> God saw that _____ was good . . .
> God called the _____ "_____."
> It was evening, and then morning—the _____ day.

Of course, there are minor variations in the use of the pattern. For example, the statement that "it was good" is lacking for the second day. Still, one could reconstruct the essentials of the *P* creation account by simply filling in the blanks for each of the six days.

The *P* author's love of ordering and organizing information is also reflected in the six day scheme of creation. As is indicated in the following chart, the creatures of days 4, 5, and 6 parallel the parts of the world which were established on days 1, 2, and 3 respectively.

DAY 1 Light *Day* and *night*	DAY 4 Luminaries for the *day* and *night*
DAY 2 Firmament (*sky*) *Waters* above and below	DAY 5 Birds in the *sky* Fishes in the *water*
DAY 3 Dry *earth* separated from sea Vegetation	DAY 6 Animals and human beings on *earth.*

Chart 2: Six Days of Creation According to *P*

The author of this narrative also uses certain specialized terms which point to a fairly sophisticated and systematic type of theological thought. The word translated "to create," for example, is the Hebrew word *bārā'* which is used only for the activity of God, and never for any kind of human creative activity. Another technical term is *mîn*, translated "kind" (in Gen 1:7, for example). It reflects an interest in categorizing nature into species. Another example occurs in the expression of Gen 2:4a, "These are the generations of heaven and earth." The word translated "generations" (it could also be translated "story") is the Hebrew *tôlĕdôt* which is a special concern of *P* that we will run across again later. Finally, though there is nothing particularly technical about this expression, we may note that the *P* author uses the Hebrew word pair *zākār* and *nĕqēbāh* for "male" and "female," respectively.

As to the way in which creation itself is understood, one of the distinctive features of the *P* account is that God creates by his word. That is, God only needs to "say" that such and such is to be, and it becomes reality. This indicates an abstract and transcendent concept of God. The *P* author does not use imagery which would picture God in too human a fashion.

Other features of the way in which creation takes place will be important when we contrast this passage with the *J* account of Gen 2:4b-3:24. For example, the situation at the beginning of creation is described in terms of a watery chaos: "The earth was a formless void with darkness covering the deeps while an awesome wind soared over the waters." To bring order out of this primeval chaos, God proceeds by *separating* (light from darkness in Gen 1:4; waters above from waters below in Gen 1:6-7; day from night in Gen 1:14; and light from darkness in Gen 1:18). As to the order in which the creatures appear, note especially that plants are created before animals, and after the animals the human race is created. It is clearly stated that the male and female are created *at the same time* (Gen 1:26-27). Yet another interesting feature is the clear indication that at first humans and animals were intended to be vegetarians as indicated by Gen 1:29-30.

Finally, we note in the *P* creation story the emphasis on the goodness of creation and the repetition of the theme of blessing (Gen 1:22; 1:28; 2:3) and the "be fertile and multiply" theme in Gen 1:22 and 1:28.

The *J* Creation Story

The discussion of the *J* creation account will be more detailed since we not only are interested in distinguishing it from the preceding *P* creation story, but we also want to make certain points which will be referred to again, later in this book. For this reason, the narrative will be treated section by section, with my own translation preceding the explanatory comments on each passage.

Gen 2:4b-7

4b When Yahweh God made the world
5   (this was before there was any shrub in the fields and before any green plants had sprouted up in the fields because Yahweh God had not made rain fall upon the earth yet and there was no man to cultivate the ground;
6   instead, a source welled up from the earth and watered the surface of the ground)
7   Yahweh God formed man from the dust of the ground and blew into his nostrils the breath of life so the man became a living being.

The structure of the passage is as follows: a temporal clause sets the scene at the time of creation, a parenthetical remark describes the conditions prevailing at that moment in the history of the universe, and finally the main clause begins the action of the story in verse 7. This structure, which is also found at the start of the *P* story and which, in fact, was a standard way to begin a creation story in the ancient world, is recognized by all modern scholars, though there is a minority opinion which would close the parentheses after verse 5 and have the main clause begin with verse 6. Taking all of verses 5 and 6 as describing the situation which existed before the creative activity of Yahweh set in, we note that it is explicitly stated that no plants exist as yet. Moreover, there is no rain and the only source of water is some kind of fountain or spring welling up from the earth. This is precisely the environment of an oasis in the desert! We see, then, that *J*'s concept of the conditions at the beginning of creation differ radically from the *P* concept of a primeval watery chaos.

The word translated "man" is Hebrew *'ādām*. This word points to the *humanity* of the creature rather than to *maleness*. Accordingly, it would be quite appropriate here to provide the more inclusive translation, "human being." However, later on in the chapter, the same Hebrew word occurs in combination with "and his wife." Since, in the latter case, *'ādām* must clearly be translated "man," consistency suggests the same translation throughout the narrative. For another view, proposed by P. Trible, see the discussion below, pp. 77-78.

In passages such as Gen 5:3, which comes from *P*, the Hebrew word *'ādām* stands for the proper name "Adam." In Gen 2:7, however, it is preceded by the definite article "the." In Hebrew, this is *hā'ādām*. Since the proper name of a person cannot be preceded by the definite article, it is apparent that the first person was just "the man," or "the human being." Nowhere does the *J* author apply the proper name "Adam." This means that it is not quite accurate to refer to the story of Gen 2-3 as the "Adam and Eve story," since "Adam" is never mentioned. Nonetheless, the assumption developed at a very early date that *hā'ādām*, "the man," was identical with *'ādām*, "Adam." We will therefore continue to use the traditional, though anachronistic, designation, "the Adam and Eve story."

In Gen 2:7, the word translated "ground" is Hebrew *'ădāmāh*. For the *J* author, the relationship between *'ādām* and *'ădāmāh* is more than just a pun. There is an intrinsic relationship between the human creature and the ground from which it comes, a relationship which, ideally, should result in mutuality and harmony. This interest in etymology is characteristic of *J*.

The Hebrew word used for the divine formation of man is a form of the verb *yāsar* which is the verb used to describe the activity of a potter in shaping clay. This human imagery contrasts with the *P* author's use of specialized theological terminology which is limited in use to describing the creative activity of God (i.e., the verb *bārā'*). After making a clay figurine in human form, Yahweh is said to *blow* into it, giving it the breath of life! Once again, we have very human characteristics and activities attributed to Yahweh. This use of human concepts in reference to God is called "anthropomorphism" from the two Greek words *anthrōpos* ("human being") and *morphē* ("form"). Anthropomorphism is one of the most striking features of the *J* work.

Gen 2:8-9

8   Then Yahweh God planted a garden in Eden, in the east, and there he placed the man that he had formed.

9   Yahweh God made sprout from the ground all the trees which are lovely to behold and good to eat. The tree of life was in the middle of the garden, also the tree of knowledge of good and bad.

The garden is planted, marking the first appearance of vegetation on the earth. According to the *J* work, this took place *after* the creation of the first human being. Note in verse 9 that it is the tree of *life* which is said to be in the middle of the garden. The present formulation of the sentence gives the impression that the tree of knowledge of good and bad is mentioned almost as an afterthought. However, in Gen 3:3 the expression "the tree which is in the middle of the garden" clearly refers to the tree of knowledge of good and bad. Therefore, some scholars believe that originally Gen 2:9 read something like, "In the middle of the garden [was] the tree of knowledge of good and bad." In this case, the mention of the tree of life would have entered into the text at the time when the tree of life theme, which comes up again in Gen 3:22, was added to the tree of knowledge theme, which is the dominant motif of the whole narrative. Whether such a combination of themes was due to the *J* author or to some other hand, either earlier or later, is debated.

Gen 2:10-14

10 Now there was a river going out from Eden. It would water the garden and afterwards it divided and became four branches.

11 The name of the first is Pishon. This is the one which winds through the whole land of Hawilah where there is gold

12 (the gold of that land is of good quality), as well as bdellium and onyx.

13 The name of the second river is Gihon. This is the one which winds through the whole land of Cush.

14 The name of the third river is Tigris. This is the one which flows by the city of Asshur. The fourth river is the Euphrates.

Apparently, the four rivers mentioned here are thought to arise from the division of the source mentioned in verse 6. This passage reminds us of a widespread mythological idea that there is a central place on the earth from which all the rivers flow. This place is sometimes identified with the dwelling place of one of the gods. Some scholars think that the author meant to be describing real geography. This is supported by the mention of the Tigris and Euphrates. The other two names, therefore, would refer to smaller rivers belonging to the Tigris-Euphrates area but impossible to identify today. Other exegetes believe that "Pishon" and "Gihon," which mean "Pusher" and "Gusher," are imaginary poetic names belonging to a never-never land rather than to real geography. This latter view receives a measure of support from the mention of the land of "Cush," which usually means Ethiopia in the Old Testament. It is obviously impossible for a river having its origins in Iraq (near the Tigris and Euphrates) to flow through Ethiopia in Africa! In any case, this little passage about the rivers is not crucial for the interpretation of the story of Adam and Eve.

Gen 2:15-17

15 Then Yahweh God took the man and placed him in the garden of Eden to cultivate it and care for it.

16 Yahweh God laid an injunction upon the man, saying, "You may eat freely from any tree in the garden,

17 but from the tree of knowledge of good and bad you shall not eat, because the moment you eat of it you will die."

An important problem in this passage concerns the exact meaning of the threat made by God. One of the traditional interpretations has been that originally Adam and Eve were intended to be immortal and the punishment threatened is that if they eat from the forbidden tree, they will become mortal and eventually die. Such a view is difficult to reconcile with Gen 3:22 where God drives Adam and Eve from the garden, saying, "Now he must not be allowed to reach out and also take from the tree of life and eat and live forever." This verse does not support the idea that they were already presumed to be immortal. Moreover, a closer examination of the wording of Gen 2:17 suggests that a more immediate death was being threatened. The phrase translated "you will die" is *môt tāmût* in Hebrew. The same phrase occurs in numerous passages in the Old Testament. For example, in 1 Kings 2:37, Solomon threatens Shimei, "The moment you go and cross the Kidron Valley, know that you shall die (*môt tāmût*)." Sure enough, when Shimei violates the king's order, he sends his hatchet man, a soldier named Benaiah, and Shimei is killed. Other parallel passages support this one in showing that *môt tāmût* refers to a punishment by execution which is to take place immediately after the transgression.

Gen 2:18-25

18 Then Yahweh God said, "It is not good that the man should be alone. Let me make for him a suitable companion."

19 So Yahweh God formed from the ground all the wild animals and all the birds of the sky and he brought

each to the man to see what he would call it. Whatever
the man would call each living being, that was its
name.

20 So the man assigned names to all the domestic animals
and all the birds of the sky and all the wild animals.
Nevertheless, no suitable companion was found for the
man.

21 So Yahweh God caused a deep sleep to fall upon the
man. While he slept, he took one of his ribs and closed
up the flesh at that spot.

22 Then Yahweh God made the rib which he had taken
from the man into a woman and brought her to the
man.

23 The man exclaimed, "At last! This one is bone of my
bones and flesh of my flesh. She shall be called
'woman' because she was taken from man."

24 This is why a man leaves his father and mother and
clings to his wife and the two of them become one
flesh.

25 Though the two of them were naked, the man and his
wife, they were not ashamed.

It is interesting to compare the Genesis account of the creation of the woman from the man's rib with the myth of the androgyne in Plato's *Symposium*. In this dialogue, Socrates and his
friends have gathered for a banquet where they are discussing
love. The comic poet Aristophanes tells a fantastic story about
the origins of the human race and of sexual attraction. He talks
about strange beings who existed long ago and who were a combination of man (Greek *andros*) and woman (Greek *gunē*) and
thus called "androgynes." He says:

> ... the primeval man was round, his back and sides
> forming a circle; and he had four hands and four feet,
> one head with two faces, looking opposite ways, set on
> a round neck and precisely alike; also four ears and two
> privy members, and the remainder to correspond. He
> could walk upright as men now do, backward or for-
> ward as he pleased, and he could also roll over and over

> at a great pace, turning on his four hands and four feet, eight in all, like tumblers going over and over with their legs in the air; this was when he wanted to run fast.[4]

These beings were perceived as a threat by the gods who therefore split them in two, each half having two legs, one face, etc. However, the divided halves were not happy with the separation:

> After the division the two parts of man, each desiring his other half, came together, and throwing their arms about one another, entwined in mutual embraces, longing to grow into one. . . . "[5]

Sexual attraction is thus explained:

> . . . the desire of one another which is implanted in us, reuniting our original nature, making one of two, and healing the state of man.[6]

Like Plato's myth of the androgyne, the story of the woman made from a part of the man explains why man and wife "cling" to one another and "become one flesh." A story which explains the origin of a striking phenomenon in this way is called an aetiology or an aetiological narrative. The *J* author was particularly fond of giving aetiologies. For example, the serpent's unusual mode of locomotion is explained as punishment for its role in the fall of Adam and Eve (Gen 3:14); the name of Noah, which means "rest" in Hebrew, is attributed to the fact that he brought rest to the human race by discovering wine (Gen 5:29 and 9:20); and the city of Babel is said to have received that name because that is where people started to "babble" in different languages (Gen 11:8-9).

It should be noticed that the search for a suitable companion for the man leads Yahweh to create *animals*. That is to say, God is experimenting! This is another example of *J*'s anthropomorphism.

The Hebrew phrase which has been translated "suitable

companion" does not imply any kind of subordination of the woman to the man. That is, God's original intention, according to the *J* author, was that the man and the woman were to be fully equal.

The last statement in the passage is that they were naked and not ashamed. This suggests that they were childlike and perhaps even unaware of their sexuality. The statement serves as a connecting link with the next scene which will lead to their discovery of shame.

Gen 3:1-7

1 Now the craftiest of all the wild animals which Yahweh God had made was the serpent. He said to the woman, "Isn't it so that God told you not to eat from any tree of the garden?"

2 The woman answered the serpent, "We may indeed eat of the fruit of the trees in the garden.

3 However, of the fruit of the tree which is in the middle of the garden, God said, 'You shall not eat of it, nor shall you touch it, lest you die.' "

4 But the serpent replied to the woman, "You will not die.

5 On the contrary, God knows that the moment you eat of it your eyes will be opened and you will become like gods knowing good and bad."

6 When the woman saw that the tree was good to eat, attractive in appearance, and that the tree was to be desired for becoming wise, she took and ate some of its fruit and also gave some to her husband who was with her and he ate.

7 Then the eyes of both of them were opened and they knew they were naked. So they sewed together fig leaves and made themselves loincloths.

This passage is frequently cited as a prime example of the *J* author's interest in psychology and his clever use of dialogue. The serpent (deliberately, it would seem) exaggerates Yahweh's prohibition and asks why they can't eat from *any* of the trees.

Once the woman begins to correct this misrepresentation, she has been hooked into the discussion and can't help wonder why, if the fruit of the other trees is permitted as food, this one tree should be off limits. Yahweh's command then begins to look arbitrary and disobedience is almost inevitable.

According to Gen 3:1, the serpent is just one of the animals "which Yahweh God had made," and not a satanic embodiment of evil. Indeed, the concept of the devil did not exist at the time of the *J* author. Furthermore, the serpent tells the truth when he says that they will not drop dead if they eat the forbidden fruit. Apparently the serpent guesses that Yahweh's mercy will prevent him from carrying through on the death penalty which had been threatened. There is an interesting parallel in 2 Samuel 12. There, the prophet Nathan tells David a story about a man who committed a grave injustice. Not realizing that he himself is the man in the story, the king is tricked into issuing the decree, "That man must die" (2 Sam 12:5). Though officially under the death sentence, just as Adam and Eve are, the king is spared by God's mercy and Nathan declares, "Yahweh has taken away your guilt; you will not die" (2 Sam 12:13). The serpent, then, is telling the truth, though it is only a partial truth. The deception consists in the fact that the serpent neglects to mention the negative results of their choice, an aspect which they will soon discover.

Note that Gen 3:3 speaks of "*the* tree in the middle of the garden" clearly meaning by this the tree of knowledge. There is no reflection here of the tree of life mentioned in Gen 2:9. We are still not clearly informed about what the tree of knowledge symbolizes, except that the kind of wisdom it confers makes one god-like. In other words, the desire for this kind of knowledge means refusal to accept the limited status of creature and represents an attempt to grasp for the prerogatives of the creator.

Gen 3:8-13

8 When they heard Yahweh God walking about the garden in the afternoon breeze, the man and his wife concealed themselves from the sight of Yahweh God among the trees of the garden.

9 Then Yahweh God called to the man and inquired of
  him, "Where are you?"

10 He answered, "I heard you in the garden and became
   fearful because I was naked, so I concealed myself."

11 He said, "Who told you that you were naked? Have
   you eaten of the tree from which I commanded you
   not to eat?"

12 The man answered, "The woman whom you put here
   with me, she is the one who gave to me from the tree
   so that I ate."

13 So Yahweh God said to the woman, "What have you
   done?" The woman replied, "The serpent led me
   astray so that I ate."

These verses contain two interesting anthropomorphisms.
First, Yahweh is said to enjoy strolling in the cool breeze of the
afternoon. Second, God is not described as knowing everything
beforehand—he discovers the disobedience of Adam and Eve by
drawing an inference from the fact that they are trying to conceal their nakedness. We are reminded of a parent figuring out
that the children have been in the cookie jar because they have
chocolate all over their faces.

This section also reflects the psychological interest of the *J*
author. Adam will not accept responsibility for his actions and
blames it on the woman "whom *you* put here with me." Eve, in
turn, blames the serpent. We could therefore take the incident
as history's first example of "passing the buck."

Gen 3:14-19

14 Then Yahweh God addressed the serpent, "Because
   you have done this, you are cursed among the animals,
   both domestic and wild. You shall crawl around on
   your belly and eat dust as long as you live.

15 Further, I will decree hostility between you and the
   woman, between your offspring and her offspring.
   They will strike at your head, while you strike at their
   heel."

16 To the woman he said, "I will greatly increase your
    suffering in pregnancy; in pain you shall bear children.
    You shall have sexual desire for your husband, but he
    will act as your master."

17 Finally, he said to the man, "Because you listened to
    your wife and ate of the tree concerning which I had
    commanded you not to eat, the ground shall be cursed
    on your account. You shall struggle to get food from it
    as long as you live.

18 It will sprout thorns and thistles for you, and you will
    eat the green plants of the field. You shall eat bread by
    the sweat of your face until you return to the ground
    from which you were taken, for you are dust and you
    shall return to dust.

The punishment of the serpent makes clear, once again,
that the text is talking about a snake and not an embodiment of
Satan. The passage provides a twofold aetiology accounting for
the snake's manner of moving about as well as the undying hostility between people and snakes. In the sentence, "They will
strike at your head while you strike at their heel," both instances
of "strike" translate the same Hebrew verb. Christian tradition
took the collective noun "offspring" as a singular referring to
the Messiah and understood the statement as a promise of his victory over the demonic forces which were the offspring of the
serpent. This interpretation finds in the text much more than
the *J* author could have intended.

The punishment of the woman affects her precisely in her
sexual roles. Childbearing, which ought to be fulfilling, will be
painful, thus introducing contradiction and alienation within
her very personal being. Moreover, her sexual desire for a man
is also a source of alienation in that it will lead to her subjugation to him as master. This sexist situation is the perversion of
the equality of the sexes willed by God according to Gen 2:18.

The punishment of the man does not directly concern his
sexuality, although it does relate to his role as provider, a role of
which one becomes fully conscious only with sexual maturity.
There should be harmony between the man (*'ādām*) and the

ground (*'ădāmāh*), not only because they sound alike, but because the first came from the latter. The called-for harmony, however, is replaced by inner contradiction, alienation, and conflict. The man will have to struggle with the soil, and it will not cooperate with his efforts.

Gen 3:20-24

20 The man gave his wife the name Eve because she became the mother of every living person.

21 Then Yahweh God made leather tunics for the man and his wife and clothed them.

22 Then Yahweh God said, "Look! The man has become like one of us, knowing good and bad. Now he must not be allowed to reach out and also take from the tree of life and eat and live forever.

23 So Yahweh God sent him away from the garden of Eden to cultivate the ground from which he had been taken.

24 He drove the man away and he stationed the cherubim and the rotating fiery sword east of the garden of Eden to guard the approach to the tree of life.

The word translated "living person" in Gen 3:20 is *ḥay*. The name of the first woman is *ḥawwāh*. Thus the *J* author explained her name on the basis of a pun which parallels the connection between *'ādām* and *'ădāmāh*.

That Yahweh makes leather tunics for Adam and Eve is probably intended as a sign of the fact that he still loves and cares for his creatures in spite of their disobedience. These leather garments are an improvement over the ineffectual loincloths they had made from fig leaves.

The tree of life is mentioned for the first time since Gen 2:9. Since this tree is apparently unknown in Gen 3:3, some scholars have suspected that the tree of life motif has been interpolated into the story about the tree of knowledge of good and bad from which it was originally distinct. In any case, it is interesting to note that the words of Yahweh in Gen 3:22 imply that it would in fact have been possible for human beings to become immortal. In view of that, we cannot help but wonder why God chose to withhold this great benefit from humankind.

Cherubim are one of a great variety of heavenly beings which the ancient Israelites believed Yahweh had at his disposal. They are depicted in ancient Near Eastern art as composite beings with the body of an animal (lion or bull), a human head, and wings. In later theology, the cherubim were thought of as a type of angel. There is no exact parallel in ancient art for the rotating fiery sword, though both swords and fire figure prominently as divine weapons in mythology.

Gen 4:1-6:4

We will deal briefly with Gen 4:1-6:4 since these chapters are not of direct interest to us in this book. The comments are limited to indicating the division of the material into *J* and *P* components.

Chapters 4 and 5 consist of genealogical materials. Some interesting facts emerge when the names in the two chapters are compared as in the following chart.

Gen 5	*Gen 4*	
Adam	Adam	
Seth	Cain (Heb. *qyn*)	Seth
Enosh	Enoch	Enosh
Kenan (Heb. *qynn*)	Irad	
Mehalalel	Mehujael	
Jared	Methusael	
Enoch	Lamech	
Methuselah		
Lamech		

Chart 3: Genealogical Lists

It will be seen that both lists have Adam, Seth and Enosh in the first three generations and both end with Lamech. They disagree in that Gen 4 has Lamech descended through the line of Cain while Gen 5 traces him through Seth, apparently ignoring the latter's brother Cain, though a variant form of that name,

Kenan, occurs in the fourth generation. Mehalalel and Mehujael seem to be variants on the same name as are Methuselah and Methusael and also Jared and Irad. Gen 5 has Enoch in the seventh generation while Gen 4 has him in the third. It turns out that all the names in the right hand column occur, sometimes in variant form, in the left hand column. The two differ as to the total number of generations involved because the list of chapter 4 puts Cain and Enoch in the same generations as Seth and Enosh respectively, whereas chapter 5 has all the names consecutively in a single line.

This comparison makes it quite clear that chapters 4 and 5 are variants of a common genealogical tradition stemming from two different sources. It is quite easy to determine that chapter 4 is *J* because of the frequent occurrence of Yahweh or LORD. On the other hand, chapter 5 begins with a reference to Elohim and the two technical terms *tôlĕdôt* ("generations") and *bārā'* ("created") which, as we have seen, all point to *P*. Once we have determined that chapter 5 is *P* on the basis of previously established criteria, we are able to see another characteristic of *P*, namely the love of using exact numbers, for example to indicate the ages of ancient patriarchs at the time they fathered their first children as well as at the times of their deaths. We can now add this predilection to our list of criteria for identifying *P*.

Though almost all of chapter 5 is *P*, there is an exception in verse 29 where the name of Noah is explained by saying, "Out of the ground which Yahweh has cursed, this one will bring us rest from our work and from the toil of our hands." This is a special kind of aetiology, explaining the meaning of a name. It points ahead to the *J* story in Gen 9:20ff. It too, therefore, must be reckoned as *J*.

Finally, we note that 6:1-4 calls God "Yahweh." It cannot, therefore, be from *P*. The simplest procedure would be to assign it to the *J* source. A number of scholars, however, regard this strange little story as a relatively late addition to the Primeval History, an addition which is not related to either *P* or *J*. We will follow this opinion in this book and hence omit the passage from consideration when we discuss the theology of the *J* author in Chapter Three.

The Flood Story (Gen 6:5-9:17)

The task of separating out the *J* and *P* versions of creation was relatively simple because the editors of the Pentateuch gave us the whole of the *P* account first, and, when that was finished, the whole of the *J* account. In the case of the flood, however, matters are considerably more complicated. At times rather short excerpts from each of the two sources were placed in close proximity. In fact, there are places where we cannot be sure exactly how to apportion the text. The literary critical process of distinguishing the *J* and *P* flood accounts is worked out in detail in the following pages in order to give the reader a clearer understanding of the methodology as well as to illustrate the fact that there are places where the Documentary Hypothesis runs into difficulties. The text is quoted from the New American Bible except that "Yahweh" has been inserted where the latter has "the LORD." The *J* portions are in roman type; the *P* portions are in italics.

*　　*　　*

Chapter 6

⁵When Yahweh saw how great was man's wickedness on earth, and how no desire that his heart conceived was ever anything but evil, ⁶he regretted that he had made man on the earth, and his heart was grieved.

a.　⁷So Yahweh said: "I will wipe out from the earth the men whom I have created, and not only the men, but also the beasts and the creeping things and the birds of the air,

---

a. This is clearly *J* since Yahweh occurs three times and there are three clear anthropomorphians: Yahweh "regretted," "his heart was grieved," and he was "sorry" that he had made the mistake of creating human beings. (When human *feelings* are attributed to God, it is technically more correct to call them "anthropopathisms" rather than "anthropomorphisms.")

for I am sorry that I made them." ⁸But Noah found favor
with Yahweh.

*⁹These are the descendants of Noah. Noah, a good man and
blameless in that age, ¹⁰for he walked with God, begot three sons:
Shem, Ham and Japheth.*

*¹¹In the eyes of God the earth was corrupt and full of lawless-
ness. ¹²When God saw how corrupt the earth had become, since all
mortals led depraved lives on earth, ¹³he said to Noah: "I have decided to put an end to all mortals on earth; the earth is full of law-
lessness because of them. So I will destroy them and all life on earth.*

*¹⁴"Make yourself an ark of gopherwood, put various compart-
ments in it, and cover it inside and out with pitch. ¹⁵This is how
you shall build it: the length of the ark shall be three hundred cu-*
b. *bits, its width fifty cubits, and its height thirty cubits. ¹⁶Make an
opening for daylight in the ark, and finish the ark a cubit above it.
Put an entrance in the side of the ark, which you shall make with
bottom, second and third decks. ¹⁷I, on my part, am about to bring
the flood [waters] on the earth, to destroy everywhere all creatures
in which there is the breath of life; everything on earth shall perish.
¹⁸But with you I will establish my covenant; you and your sons,
your wife and your sons' wives, shall go into the ark. ¹⁹Of all other
living creatures you shall bring two into the ark, one male and one
female, that you may keep them alive with you.*

²⁰Of all kinds of birds, of all kinds of beasts, and of all kinds

---

b. Verses 11-13 duplicate the information already given in verses
5-8. In this doublet, however, Elohim is used instead of Yahweh. Moreover, we find a characteristic *P* word, *tôlĕdôt* ("descendants"), and a total absence of anthropomorphism (or, anthropopathism). This is
doubtless *P.*

In verses 14-18, there are not very many clear signs which
would point to *J* or *P.* There is, of course, the presence of specific numbers in v. 15—a feature we associate with *P.* The principal reason for
attributing the whole passage to *P* is that it is clearly *P* at the beginning
and at the end with no apparent breaks or discontinuities in between.

Note that it is very clear in verse 19 that according to *P* there
are to be two and only two of each kind of animal. The expression for
"male and female" is the same one employed by *P* in 1:27, i.e., *zākār* and
nĕqēbāh.

of creeping things, two of each shall come into the ark with you, to stay alive. ²¹*Moreover, you are to provide yourself with all the food that is to be eaten, and store it away, that it may serve as provisions for you and for them.*" ²²*This Noah did; he carried out all the commands that God gave him.*

Chapter 7

¹Then Yahweh said to Noah: "Go into the ark, you and all your household, for you alone in this age have I found to
c. be truly just. ²Of every clean animal, take with you seven pairs, a male and its mate; and of the unclean animals, one pair, a male and its mate; ³likewise, of every clean bird of the

---

c. The Yahweh in 7:1 tells us immediately that we are beginning a *J* passage. The *J* account distinguishes clean and unclean animals. For our purposes, we can understand the category of clean animals simply as those animals which are fit for human consumption. The *P* author did not make the distinction between clean and unclean, because in his mind people were all *vegetarians* at this time (see above, comment on p. 10, and discussion of 9:3-6, below). The *J* author specifically requires the presence of seven pairs of the clean animals. There is outright contradiction of the *P* view that there were only two of each. Of course, we can understand why *J* thought there must have been more of the clean animals: he did not know anything about a primitive vegetarianism and believed that the people on the ark were eating meat. If there had been just one pair of the clean animals, it is precisely the clean species which would have died out!

On two occassions in 7:2, we have the expression "a male and its mate" which is *'îš wĕ'ištô* in Hebrew. This is similar to *J* expressions in chapters 2-3 and contrasts with the *zākār* and *nĕqēbāh* characteristic of *P*. In verse 3, however, *zākār* and *nĕqēbāh* do occur. Either we must presume a slip-up on the part of an editor who would have inadvertently used the *P* expression in a *J* context, or we must conclude that *zākār* and *nĕqēbāh* were occasionally used by *J* and so are not an infallible criterion of *P*.

Note that according to 7:1-4 (i.e., according to *J*), Noah and his family were to enter the ark seven days before the beginning of the disaster. That disaster, moreover, is specified as consisting of rain. The rain will fall for forty days and forty nights.

air, seven pairs, a male and a female, and of all the unclean birds, one pair, a male and a female. Thus you will keep their issue alive over all the earth. ⁴Seven days from now I will bring rain down on the earth for forty days and forty nights, and so I will wipe out from the surface of the earth every moving creature that I have made." ⁵Noah did just as Yahweh had commanded him.

d.   ⁶*Noah was six hundred years old when the flood waters came upon the earth.* ⁷Together with his sons, his wife, and his sons'
e. wives, Noah went into the ark because of the waters of the flood. ⁸Of the clean animals and the unclean, of the birds,
f. *and of everything that creeps on the ground,* ⁹[*two by two*] *male and female entered the ark with Noah,* just as Yahweh had com-
g. manded him. ¹⁰As soon as the seven days were over, the waters of the flood came upon the earth.

          ¹¹*In the six hundredth year of Noah's life, in the second*
h. *month, on the seventeenth day of the month: it was on that day that*

---

d. The exact ages point this out as a *P* section.

e-g. Sections e to g illustrate the kinds of difficulties one may encounter in working out the division of sources. Verses 7 and 10 harmonize with the *J* ideas of section c that the ark was boarded seven days before the start of the rain. This duplicates and contradicts the statement of 7:13 (*P*) that they entered the ark on the exact same day as the start of the flood. So verses 7 and 10 seem to be *J*. Furthermore, the distinction of clean and unclean animals in the beginning of verse 8 also fits in with *J*. On the other hand, the idea that there were just *two* of each kind of animal is the *P* version. Moreover, "male and female" (*zā-kār* and *něqēbāh*) seem to belong to P, as does the term "everything that creeps." These comments will explain why the sections e to g have been assigned as indicated above. Admittedly, there is some awkwardness here. Perhaps this is due to the way in which the editors worked, not always preserving a clear distinction between their *P* source and their *J* source.

h. The exact age, as well as the exact date, is characteristic of *P*. (In fact, the calendar which gave *numbers* rather than *names* to the months was a peculiarity of the priests which can now be reconstructed on the basis of evidence in the Dead Sea Scrolls.) The cause of the flood,

> *All the fountains of the great abyss burst forth,*
> *and the floodgates of the sky were opened.*

i.   ¹²For forty days and forty nights heavy rain poured down on the earth.

¹³*On the precise day named, Noah and his sons Shem, Ham and Japheth, and Noah's wife, and the three wives of Noah's sons had entered the ark,* ¹⁴*together with every kind of wild beast, every*
j. *kind of domestic animal, every kind of creeping thing of the earth, and every kind of bird.* ¹⁵*Pairs of all creatures in which there was the breath of life entered the ark with Noah.* ¹⁶*Those that entered were male and female and of all species they came, as God had com-*
k. *manded Noah.* Then Yahweh shut him in.

l.   ¹⁷The flood continued upon the earth for forty days. *As the waters increased, they lifted the ark, so that it rose above the earth.* ¹⁸*The swelling waters increased greatly, but the ark floated*
m. *on the surface of the waters.* ¹⁹*Higher and higher above the earth rose the waters, until all the highest mountains everywhere were submerged,* ²⁰*the crest rising fifteen cubits higher than the submerged mountains.* ²¹*All creatures that stirred on earth perished:*

---

according to *P*, is not rain, but the collapse of the universe. In chapter 1, *P* had talked about the *separation* of the waters above from the waters below. Here, the creative process is reversed and there is a return to the chaotic situation of pre-creation times. In the *P* understanding, this appears to have been a virtually instantaneous process so that the height of the flood waters are reached the first day, not after forty days and nights.

i. The number forty and the mention of rain point to *J*.

j. The exact dates point to P. Note the contradiction with the *J* views found in sections c, e, and g.

k-l. The name Yahweh and the anthropomorphism point to *J*, as does the number forty.

m. There are not many clues here. However, because of the absence of rain, and the impression that the increasing waters are due to the collapse of the cosmic structure mentioned under h, we suspect *P*. Note also the exact number in v. 20.

birds, cattle, wild animals, and all that swarmed on the earth, as well as all mankind. ²²Everything on dry land with the faintest breath of life in its nostrils died. out. ²³Yahweh wiped

n. out every living thing on earth: man and cattle, the creeping things and the birds of the air; all were wiped out from the earth. Only Noah and those with him in the ark were left.

Chapter 8

²⁴*The waters maintained their crest over the earth for one hundred and fifty days,* ¹*and then God remembered Noah and all*

o. *the animals, wild and tame, that were with him in the ark. So God made a wind sweep over the earth, and the waters began to subside.* ²*The fountains of the abyss and the floodgates of the sky were*

p. *closed,* and the downpour from the sky was held back. ³Gradually the waters receded from the earth. *At the end of one hundred and fifty days, the waters had so diminished* ⁴*that, in the*

q. *seventh month, on the seventeenth day of the month, the ark came to rest on the mountains of Ararat.* ⁵*The waters continued to diminish until the tenth month, and on the first day of the tenth month the tops of the mountains appeared.*

⁶At the end of forty days Noah opened the hatch he had made in the ark, ⁷and he sent out a raven, to see if the waters had lessened on the earth. It flew back and forth until the waters dried off from the earth. ⁸Then he sent out a dove, to

---

n. This duplicates information in m and has Yahweh; therefore it is *J*.

o. The chronology involving one hundred and fifty, rather than seven or forty, is part of *P*. The first part of verse 2 repairs the cosmic damage mentioned in section h. Elohim occurs twice. The sweeping wind of verse 1 suggests the mighty wind of Gen 1:2 (*P*).

p. This duplicates information already given by *P*. The "downpour" (= rain) points to *J*.

q. The number one hundred and fifty and the exact dates point to *P*.

see if the waters had lessened on the earth. ⁹But the dove
could find no place to alight and perch, and it returned to
r. him in the ark, for there was water all over the earth. Putting out his hand, he caught the dove, and drew it back to
him inside the ark. ¹⁰He waited seven days more and again
sent the dove out from the ark. ¹¹In the evening the dove
came back to him, and there in its bill was a plucked-off olive
leaf! So Noah knew that the waters had lessened on the
earth. ¹²He waited still another seven days and then released
the dove once more; and this time it did not come back.

¹³In the six hundred and first year of Noah's life, in the first
s. *month, on the first day of the month, the water began to dry up on*
t. *the earth.* Noah then removed the covering of the ark and saw
that the surface of the ground was drying up. *¹⁴In the second*
month, on the twenty-seventh day of the month, the earth was dry.

¹⁵Then God said to Noah: ¹⁶"Go out of the ark, together with
your wife and your sons and your sons' wives. ¹⁷Bring out with
you every living thing that is with you—all bodily creatures, be
they birds or animals or creeping things of the earth—and let them
u. *abound on the earth, breeding and multiplying on it." ¹⁸So Noah*
came out, together with his wife and his sons and his sons' wives;
¹⁹and all the animals, wild and tame, all the birds, and all the
creeping creatures of the earth left the ark, one kind after another.

²⁰Then Noah built an altar to Yahweh, and choosing
from every clean animal and every clean bird, he offered ho-
locausts on the altar. ²¹When Yahweh smelled the sweet

---

r. The forty days point to J. According to *J*, Noah had to experi-
ment in order to determine when he could get out of the ark. According to the *P* section of 14-16 (i.e., section u) Noah leaves the ark when
God tells him to.

s. The exact date points to *P*.

t. The covering seems to refer back to the *J* section k.

u. This has an exact date, the use of Elohim, and the theme of
"breeding and multiplying," all characteristics of *P*.

odor, he said to himself: "Never again will I doom the earth because of man, since the desires of man's heart are evil from the start; nor will I ever again strike down all living beings,
v. as I have done.

> ²²As long as the earth lasts,
>   seedtime and harvest,
>   cold and heat,
> Summer and winter,
>   and day and night
>   shall not cease."

Chapter 9

¹God blessed Noah and his sons and said to them: "Be fertile and multiply and fill the earth. ²Dread fear of you shall come upon all the animals of the earth and all the birds of the air, upon all the creatures that move about on the ground and all the fishes of the sea; into your power they are delivered. ³Every creature that is alive shall be yours to eat; I give them all to you as I did the green plants. ⁴Only flesh with its lifeblood still in it you shall not eat. ⁵For your own lifeblood, too, I will demand an accounting: from
w. *every animal I will demand it, and from man in regard to his fellow man I will demand an accounting for human life.*

---

v. The passage uses Yahweh. Moreover, it mentions sacrifice. According to the priestly system, sacrifice was not legitimate until the proper way of offering it was revealed, along with the appointment of the valid priestly line, in the time of Moses. There is never any mention of sacrifice in the *P* work before the time of Moses.

Reading about this sacrifice, we learn an additional reason why the *J* author thought there was more than one pair of clean animals on the ark: the species would have died out when one or both of them were sacrificed by Noah!

Note also the powerful anthropomorphism "Yahweh smelled the sweet odor." Compare 8:21 and 6:5-7. The very reason which caused God to send the flood in the first place now becomes the reason for never sending another flood!

w. There are many clues to *P* in this passage. Elohim occurs repeatedly. There is the "be fertile and multiply" theme. There is a

> *⁶If anyone sheds the blood of man,*
> *by man shall his blood be shed;*
> *For in the image of God*
> *has man been made.*

> *⁷Be fertile, then, and multiply; abound on earth and subdue it."*
> *⁸God said to Noah and to his sons with him: ⁹"See, I am now estab-*
> *lishing my covenant with you and your descendants after you*
> *¹⁰and with every living creature that was with you: all the birds,*
> *and the various tame and wild animals that were with you and*
> *came out of the ark. ¹¹I will establish my covenant with you, that*
> *never again shall all bodily creatures be destroyed by the waters of*
> *a flood; there shall not be another flood to devastate the earth."*
> *(The P material continues through verse 17.)*

Gen 9:18-11:27

After having worked through the evidence for the division of the flood story into its two sources, the reader should have a good feel for the process involved and be at least partly convinced that it is reasonable to analyze the material in this way. It will not be necessary to do a detailed separation of sources for the remainder of the Primeval History. Nonetheless, we need to summarize the results yielded by such an analysis according to the consensus of literary critics.

The story of Noah and his sons in Gen 9:18-27 is universally recognized as belonging to *J*, while the concluding verses of the chapter (9:28-29) bear the marks of *P*. The genealogical material in chapter 10 is a combination of *J* and *P*. It is generally agreed that verses 8-19, 21 and 24-39 are *J* while the remainder is *P*. In chapter 11 the Tower of Babel story (Gen 11:1-9) is clearly *J* while the genealogy in 11:10-27 is *P*. In 11:28-32 there is a combination of *J* and *P*.

---

change in the dietary restrictions which had been mentioned in 1:29-30. Finally, the expression "to establish a covenant" found in 9:9 is a theme which occurs often in *P* materials later on (e.g., Gen 17:7 and Exod 6:4).

Conclusion

Now that we have discussed the way in which the work of
the *J* author can be recovered from the present biblical text, we
will go on to examine some Babylonian mythological materials
and then discuss the theology of the *J* author. Having examined
these broader contexts, we will be well prepared to deal with
the meaning of the Adam and Eve story of Gen 2-3.

Notes

1. While the Elohim passages *never* employ Yahweh, the Yahweh
passages occasionally use Elohim or the combination Yahweh-Elohim.
This is why the word "prefer" is used in the above sentence. Note also
that earlier Christian scholars thought this special name of God was
pronounced "Jehovah." It is now agreed that Yahweh, not Jehovah, is
the correct form.

2. For a brief and readable introduction, see N. Habel, *Literary
Criticism of the Old Testament* (Philadelphia: Fortress Press, 1971).

3. The division of the Hebrew Bible into verses is *not* part of its
ancient form and does not appear, for example, in the Dead Sea Scrolls,
manuscripts which were written roughly at the time of Christ. The tra-
ditionists who introduced verse divisions at a relatively late date occasionally, as in this example, put the division at a point which does not
correspond to modern critical analysis.

4. B. Jowett (trans.), *Plato's Symposium* (Indianapolis: Bobbs-Mer-
rill, 1956) 30-31.

5. *Ibid.*, 32.

6. *Ibid.*

Chapter Two

Babylonian Myths Related to Genesis 1-11

There are two principal reasons for examining the Babylonian mythological texts which are discussed in this chapter. The first, more general, objective is to establish a positive appreciation for the contribution made by myth. More specifically, the Babylonian materials provide us with some insights into the nature of the original sources upon which the biblical authors were dependent.

It is necessary to develop a positive appreciation of the nature and meaning of myth, because in our culture the word "myth" is often understood as meaning something which is obviously untrue and in which it is rather naive and unsophisticated to believe. However, when we look at the myths of so-called primitive peoples, including those which have come down to us in ancient texts, it is clear that a more positive understanding of myth is required. While the myths usually do not represent objective and factual truth, they do grapple with some of the profound questions of human existence in the form of story and symbol. While not all myths are equally true, we must nonetheless recognize that there is truth in myth. Indeed, myth can often express the truth in a deeper and more powerful way than is possible by the use of scientific language.

The discussion contained in this chapter aims not only to

promote a more favorable attitude toward myth, but also to
show that the biblical stories are to some extent based upon pre-
existing literary traditions. In some cases, notably regarding the
flood story, the Genesis account is very close to the Babylonian
prototype and we can be quite confident that we know where
the biblical authors got their information. In other cases, the
parallels are not as precise. We can see that certain themes as
well as the way of dealing with the themes are common to the
two cultures. This helps us to understand and interpret the biblical stories, even though we do not have an exact model upon
which the Genesis accounts might have been based. In any case
it must be insisted that even where the biblical stories are most
clearly dependent upon Babylonian sources, there are important
differences. For while the biblical authors took over the older
traditions which had come down to them, they made important
modifications intended to bring the stories into harmony with
their own Israelite theology. In fact, the biblical version sometimes appears to be deliberately designed to *deny* religious
claims made by the older stories told among their neighbors.
Close attention to both similarities and differences is required if
we are to attain an adequate understanding of these texts.

The *Gilgamesh Epic*[1]

The *Gilgamesh Epic* is universally recognized as being one of
the greatest works of literature to have come down to us from
ancient times. After having lain buried in ancient ruins for centuries, this work was recovered by archaeologists since the middle of the nineteenth century. The fullest copies, inscribed on
clay tablets during the seventh century B.C., were discovered in
the library founded by the Assyrian king Ashurbanipal at Nineveh. Also, there are substantial fragments of the work from the
Old Babylonian period, that is, the dynasty whose most famous
king was Hammurapi (about 1700 B.C.). The epic as we now
have it appears to have been composed during the Old Babylonian Period, though it adapts and links together older tales
which had circulated in Sumerian during the previous millenni-
um. The Gilgamesh material, then, was very popular through-

out Mesopotamia for a long period of time. It was also known outside of Mesopotamia. The site of Boghazköy in modern Turkey has yielded fragments of the Babylonian version as well as Hittite and Hurrian translations. Smaller fragments from archaeological sites in Syria and Palestine underline the wide diffusion of the work in antiquity and its currency in the intellectual milieu which gave birth to the Bible.

The hero of the story is Gilgamesh, king of Uruk, a man who actually existed, though the stories told about him are, for the most part, legendary. As the story opens, we learn that the citizens of Uruk are unhappy with their king because his excessive zeal for activity leaves no peace to the city. They cry to the gods for help. An assembly of the major deities is convened in heaven and they decide upon a strategem designed to relieve the distress of Uruk's citizens: one of the goddesses will create a man named Enkidu who is the equal of Gilgamesh in size and strength. When they become friends, Gilgamesh will have another outlet for his energy and will leave his subjects in comparative peace.

The story of Enkidu is very interesting in its own right and constitutes a major subplot of the overall epic. At his creation, he is said to be a very hairy being. This is a sign of being wild and uncivilized. He lives on the semi-arid steppe, running with the gazelles, eating grass, and drinking at the watering holes with the animals who are his friends. Within the overall epic, he is not, of course, the first man, since Gilgamesh and the people of Uruk already exist. Nonetheless, the story of Enkidu and what happens to him appears to be an ancient way of talking about how the human race made the transition from a state of harmony with nature and the animals to the civilized existence which was actually experienced. On another level, Enkidu embodies the simplicity and innocence of childhood. As such, he is comparable to Adam in paradise before the fall.

The events which lead to Enkidu's estrangement from the animals begin to unfold because he is in the habit of helping the animals to escape the traps set for them by hunters. The latter enlist the aid of a prostitute from Uruk in carrying out an age-old plot to bring about Enkidu's downfall: she is to wait by his favorite watering hole, and when he comes, she will expose herself in order to attract him. The conspiracy succeeds in extraordinary fashion: Enkidu has intercourse with the prostitute for six days and seven nights! When he attempts to return to the gazelles, a note of sadness enters the story: they reject him and turn away from him. He tries to chase after them, but he has lost his former speed and cannot catch up. He has become alienated from the world of the animals.

Realizing that an important change has come over him, Enkidu has no choice but to return to the prostitute. She tells him that he has become wise and is now like a god. These are very interesting concepts reflecting ancient convictions that sexuality, especially within a religious context, provided an avenue to knowledge and to communion with the world of the gods. This also throws light upon the promise of the serpent in Gen 3:5 that eating the fruit of the forbidden tree will make them "like gods, knowing good and bad." The significance of this parallel for interpreting Genesis 2-3 will be discussed later.

The woman now becomes Enkidu's teacher as he sits at her feet for instruction. She then assumes the role of mother as she clothes him with some of her own garments and takes him by the hand, leading him to the abode of the shepherds—a kind of half-way station between the wilderness native to Enkidu and the city of Uruk which is his ultimate destination. Among the shepherds, Enkidu is introduced to strange new food and drink. He who was accustomed to eat grass is presented with bread. The nature boy who sucked milk from the gazelles' udders is offered beer. Never one to do things in a small way, he drinks seven kegs. His face beams as he realizes he is well on his way to becoming a man.

The initiation of Enkidu is completed when the prostitute takes him to Uruk where he meets Gilgamesh. The two heroes become fast friends and resolve, after some debate, to go on a dangerous expedition to the cedar forest. The absence of Gilgamesh from Uruk is apparently the answer to the prayers of its citizens, who had felt overtaxed by the energetic demands of their young king.

When Enkidu and Gilgamesh debate the advisability of set-ting off for the cedar forest, we learn something very important about Gilgamesh's attitude to death. Enkidu has warned that the cedar forest is guarded by a terrible monster named Huwawa (Humbaba in the Assyrian version). Gilgamesh, on the other hand, belittles his friend for the latter's timidity. Gilgamesh believes that life is so ephemeral that there is no point in fretting over it. "Why fear death?" he argues, since it is the lot of all men. If they fall in battle with the monster of the cedar forest, at least they will achieve immortal fame.

At this point in the story, then, Gilgamesh exhibits the attitude of the brash young warrior, arrogant in self-confidence, and scoffing at death. Later on, we will see his attitude change.

The two mighty friends set out on their great adventure. They do indeed kill Huwawa and bring back timbers from the cedar forest. As the people of Uruk celebrate the accomplishments of their mighty king, his beauty and splendor are so impressive that the goddess Ishtar falls in love and proposes to him. Not only does Gilgamesh reject the invitation of the goddess, he thoroughly insults her. In revenge, she arranges to have the "Bull of Heaven" sent against Enkidu and Gilgamesh. Undaunted, the two heroes kill the bull and hurl a piece of its flesh at Ishtar, saying that they would gladly do the same to her if they could. This insult to a deity is unbearable. The gods decide that one of the two must die because of the offense. The death sentence falls upon Enkidu.

As he lies upon his death bed, Enkidu reflects upon his life experience. Has his transition from childlike simplicity to maturity, from harmony with nature to civilization been worth it? Had he not been better off when he ran with the gazelles? "Definitely," he concludes at first, as he curses all the persons who were involved with his initiation and fall—especially the prostitute. But the sun god, the epitome of fairness and objectivity, points out the other side of the coin. As a result of his experience, Enkidu has been introduced to human food, he has enjoyed sleeping on a bed rather than on the ground, and he has benefited from the friendship of a fellow human being. Moreover, now that he is dying, he can be assured that his companion will provide him with a fine funeral! Enkidu recognizes the truth in what he has been told, and he balances his previous curse with a blessing.

It is important to realize at this point that in the ancient Near East, as in folk literature throughout the world, a word of blessing or curse, once uttered, can never be retracted. The curse he has pronounced on the prostitute and on others cannot be withdrawn. It can, however, be mitigated by a word of blessing which restores balance and equity.

This scene, in which Enkidu reflects upon his experience, may be regarded as the epic's way of dealing with the question of civilization. Were we better off when we were in harmony with nature, when we ran with the gazelles? Is the simplicity and innocence of childhood preferable to the complexities and ambiguities of adulthood? The *Gilgamesh Epic* answers these questions in a balanced and nuanced fashion: though some things have been lost, other things have been gained. The epic thus reflects a profound understanding of the ambiguities involved in the process of growth. The awareness of one's sexuality and the responsibilities which that entails is gained at the expense of childlike innocence and freedom. Technological advance takes place along with the loss of community with nature and the world of the animals. The "fall" of Enkidu was inevitable, but it elicits in us feelings of loss, pathos, and nostalgia.

With the death of Enkidu, a major change comes over Gilgamesh. The arrogant young warrior who scoffed at death is overwhelmed when his friend dies. He is terrified, obsessed by the threat of death and determined to set out on a heroic journey in search of immortality. He goes in search of his ancestor Utnapishtim, the Babylonian Noah, who had been made immortal after the great flood. Perhaps Utnapishtim will reveal to him the secret of immortal life.

Gilgamesh undertakes the difficult journey in search of Utnapishtim and immortality. After struggling though great difficulties, he reaches the end of the world where he encounters an innkeeper named Siduri. She is appalled at the physical condition of Gilgamesh and asks why he has submitted himself to such unbearable hardships. He tells her of his friendship with Enkidu and the trauma he experienced at his companion's

death. He now wishes to find Utnapishtim and the secret of immortality. Siduri advises him that his quest is in vain. When the
gods created mankind, they assigned death as our fate. We
should accept that. Gilgamesh should return to his city and enjoy the ordinary pleasures available to us humans: to bathe and
put on festive attire; to rejoice in good food and drink; to take
pleasure in intimacy with one's wife and delight in the loving
gaze of one's children. As long as Gilgamesh is engaged in the
hopeless effort to achieve an impossible goal, he is missing out
on the only pleasures which are possible for humankind.

Needless to say, Gilgamesh will not hear of the common
sense advice provided by Siduri. He continues on his journey
and reaches the place where Utnapishtim lives. He asks his ancestor how it happened that he became immortal. At this point
Utnapishtim relates the story of the flood. The story is essentially the same as that contained in Genesis 6-9.[2] A decision has
been made in heaven to destroy the human race by flood. One
chosen man receives a divine revelation telling him of the coming flood and instructing him to build a ship of specified dimen-
sions, coated with pitch to make it waterproof. After
representatives of the different kinds of animals have come
aboard, the entrance is sealed and the flood rains begin. All human life perishes, except for the persons fortunate enough to be
on the ship with Utnapishtim. When the flood waters begin to
recede, the boat settles on the top of a mountain in the north.
The flood hero releases a bird to see whether it will find a dry
place to land or return to the ship because everything is still cov-
ered with water. Finally, after several repetitions of this experi-
ment, the bird does not return. The flood hero then comes out
of the ship and offers sacrifice to the gods.

There can be no doubt that the biblical story of the flood
was based upon a Babylonian original which was either identical with or very similar to the flood account found in the *Gilgamesh Epic*. Of course there are some important differences
between the biblical and the Babylonian versions, some of
which will be discussed below. The one difference which is relevant at this point of our discussion of the *Gilgamesh Epic* is that
in the Bablylonian version, the flood hero (Utnapishtim) was

made immortal after the flood. This is why Gilgamesh had traveled to the abode of Utnapishtim in the first place. Unfortunately for Gilgamesh, however, Utnapishtim tells him that the gift of immortality had been conferred under very special circumstances which could not be duplicated. There is no chance that Gilgamesh too could become immortal.

Apparently resigned to this discouraging state of affairs, Gilgamesh prepares to return to Uruk. As he is about to leave, however, Utnapishtim's wife encourages her husband to tell Gilgamesh about the thorny bush, found at the bottom of the sea, which can effect rejuvenation. Gilgamesh acts on this information, dives to the bottom of the sea, and gains possession of this magical plant. What he has obtained is not, of course, as good as immortality. Nonetheless it is quite a good second best. After he has become old he can, presumably by eating the fruit of this bush, become young again. With this treasure in hand, he sets out for his home in Uruk.

On the way, he traverses hot dry desert areas. When he sees an inviting pond of cool, refreshing water, he stops to bathe. Carelessly, he leaves the magical plant unguarded at the edge of the water as he bathes. A *snake* comes along, eats the plant, and sheds its skin (i.e., attains rejuvenation). Gilgamesh is overcome with grief and bemoans the fact that all of his great struggles and hardships were for nothing.

From this point on, the epic rushes very quickly to its end. In fact the ending is so abrupt that experts cannot agree about its significance. Gilgamesh returns to the city of Uruk and begins praising the beauty of the city. The best interpretation seems to be that he is somehow buoyed up by his return to Uruk. Though he has not found immortality, he has undergone an inner personal change. He can once again enter into responsible social interaction with other human beings, taking up his role as king, and finding meaning and purpose in life even though immortality was beyond his grasp.

The events in the *Gilgamesh Epic* are not factual. We find imaginative material from the world of myth and epic. That does not mean, however, that this great work of literature is devoid of meaning and truth. It deals with some very basic human

questions. Is the innocence of childhood preferable to the ambi-
guity of adulthood and maturity? Was the human race better off
before the rise of civilization, when men lived in harmony with
nature and the animals? How should we react to the fact that we
must die? Is it better to accept the limitations of our human situation, as does Siduri? Or is the nobler course to rebel and strive
against the fate as does Gilgamesh?

Not only does the *Gilgamesh Epic* deal with important questions, it provides wise solutions to some of the problems it deals
with. It regards the "fall" from childhood to adulthood as an ambiguous experience which entails gains as well as losses. The
same applies to the "fall" from the paradise of nature into civilization. Though the process of growth is necessary and desirable,
it entails the loss of an innocence which seems lovely to us and
for which we experience a kind of nostalgia.

The *Gilgamesh Epic* also embodies a measure of universal
truth in its handling of the problem of death. All of us must go
through a process analogous to the experience of Gilgamesh. In
youth we may ignore, even scoff at, the prospect of death. At
some point its inevitable reality strikes home. We seek ways of
making ourselves immortal through various kinds of achievement. We rebel against its grim reality and believe that by our
striving we can escape its clutches. But if the process of growth
comes full circle, we learn to accept the fact that we must die
and gain the strength and the wisdom to lead a purposeful and
meaningful life even in the face of death.

What I am suggesting, then, is that while this story is "fic-
tional," it is not thereby false. For in the experience of Enkidu
and Gilgamesh, we learn the truth about ourselves.

In the introduction to this chapter, I indicated a twofold objective of establishing a positive appreciation for myth as well as
uncovering some of the specific sources upon which the biblical
authors drew. We have already touched upon the second objective by pointing out the relationship between the biblical and
Babylonian flood stories. Later in this volume, I will discuss the
more remote but no less real connection between the stories of
Enkidu and Adam. For in both cases we are dealing with "primeval" man who lived in a paradise of peace and harmony with

nature. After an encounter with a woman, this man experienced a "fall" into adulthood and civilization—that is, life as we actually know it. There are other thematic connections too. The idea that eating from the fruit of the Tree of Life or the bush of rejuvenation can counteract old age and death binds the two stories together. Finally, the role of the snake in the *Gilgamesh Epic* and in Genesis 3 is striking. While the specific details of the snake's intervention vary, it is nonetheless due to the serpent's appearance that man (both Adam and Gilgamesh) is forced to face up to the reality of his mortality.

The *Atrahasis Epic*

As early as 1872, a number of pieces from among the thousands of tablets and fragments recovered from Ashurbanipal's palace in Nineveh were identified as belonging to a Babylonian version of the flood story. It was not until almost a hundred years later, however, that scholars were able to piece together the many fragments coming from different archaeological sites and stored in different museums into the fairly coherent whole which is now known as the *Atrahasis Epic*. About one-third of the total text is still missing, but enough survives for us to be able to reconstruct the main lines of the narrative. In addition to the fragments from Nineveh, substantial parts are found on tablets from the Old Babylonian period excavated in ancient Sippar, about twenty-five miles southwest of modern Baghdad. There are other fragments, among them one from Ras Shamra (ancient Ugarit) on the coast of Syria. The text was therefore well known in antiquity, though apparently not as popular as the *Gilgamesh Epic*. The composition of the *Atrahasis Epic* is dated to the same general period of history as the composition of *Gilgamesh*, though *Atrahasis* is perhaps a little older.[3]

The story begins at a time before the creation of the human race. Strange as it may seem to us, the Babylonians believed that even in those early times, agricultural work had been necessary. They thought that the gods depended upon the products of agriculture for their food. Therefore, in the primeval times with which the narrative opens, there existed a class of worker gods who performed the agricultural labor. We learn, however, that these gods resented the hard labor which they were forced to do and rebelled. They burned their tools and gathered angrily around the house of Enlil, who was the overseer of the labor.

Enlil did not know how to solve the problem of the rebellion of the worker gods. He summoned the other gods to advise him and a solution was proposed. The male deity Enki would team up with the mother goddess to produce an invention that would satisfy all the gods. The solution was to create human beings!

The process of creating men and women consisted essentially in making clay statues which were set aside to incubate for a period of nine days, after which they came to life. An interesting detail of the story is that one of the gods, presumably the leader of the worker gods in their rebellion, was killed, and his flesh and blood were mixed with the clay from which humans were made. The human heartbeat is then explained as a kind of funeral drum which beats perpetually in memory of the god who gave his life to make the creation of humankind possible.

With this clever invention to do the work, all of the gods were free to retire to heaven. After a period of 1,200 years, however, a flaw in the invention of Enki and the mother goddess became apparent: they multiplied uncontrollably and became too numerous. With the large number came a large amount of noise. In fact humans were so noisy that the god Enlil was unable to sleep. As a result, he resolved to destroy the human race in order to have peace and quiet. In collaboration with one of the other gods, he sent disease to ravage humanity and destroy it. Fortunately for mankind, however, the god Enki came to Atrahasis and revealed a plan which would bring an end to the death-dealing plague. The plan worked and the human race was saved—for the time being, at least.

After another 1,200 years, their number had grown again and once more the tumultuous result impeded Enlil's rest. He tried for a second time to wipe out the noisy human race, but again Enki intervened in a revelation to Atrahasis and helped save humanity.

This little scenario was replayed a number of times. We are

not sure exactly how many times the cycle was repeated because parts of the clay tablets are broken. In any case, the time came when Enlil wanted to resolve this problem once and for all. He obtained the agreement of the other gods that a flood was to be sent to destroy all life on earth. He demanded that the gods swear to keep the plan a secret so that no mortal would survive the disaster. Enki, however, used a trick to get around his oath and he provided Atrahasis with the information that the flood was coming and that he should build an ark to save himself. There follows a detailed account of the flood whcih is essentially the same as we saw already in the *Gilgamesh Epic*, although the *Atrahasis* version adds some interesting new details. One of these new details is the information that the flood caused suffering to the gods! For in wiping out the human race, they were destroying the creatures who substituted for the worker gods, and so the gods were left without any food. The story treats the gods in an almost burlesque fashion. We read that they gathered to the feeding trough, crowding like sheep, but found it empty. And they end up doubled over from hunger cramps. No wonder that the gods swarmed like flies over the sacrifice offered by Atrahasis when he emerged from the ark: it was the first time they had had food since the beginning of the flood.

At the end of the flood, there is an interesting scene where some of the other gods severely rebuke Enlil for having sent the flood. He is told that the flood was an excessively severe measure that was unfair and uncalled for. Enlil retorts that he was only trying to solve a problem which was caused by Enki and the mother goddess when they invented this creature that multiplied too rapidly. He challenges them to solve this problem. The solution they come up with, and which brings an end to the story, is to institute certain natural and social phenomena which will keep the human population down. In the realm of nature there are to be some women who are barren, and some babies will be still-born. On the social plane, there will now be various religious communities of women who will not have children because, for example, they are committed to perpetual virginity. So we see that these natural and social phenomena were regarded by the Babylonians of historical times as measures designed by the gods to prevent overpopulation.

The *Atrahasis Epic* illustrates very powerfully the way in which myth incorporates and expresses a civilization's basic understanding of the nature of humankind, its place in the universe, and its relationship to the gods. From the circumstances that lead to creation, we see that the Babylonians understood the essence of human nature as being servants of the gods, providing the gods with the necessities of life by doing the work which the gods themselves did not want to do. This concept of humans as the slaves or servants of the gods is found in many religions, including Christianity and Judaism. But in the *Atrahasis Epic* it receives a particularly concrete and literal significance. The role of humanity as servants, however, does not mean that they are abject and subservient. The dignity of the human race is enhanced by the fact that the gods need humanity. The functioning of the whole cosmos, then, is dependent upon a human contribution. The high status of humankind is reinforced by the idea that the flesh and blood of a god went into the substance of which we are made. Our heartbeats are a constant reminder that there is something divine in all of us.

If we are fair and open-minded about it, we must recognize that there is a measure of truth in the *Atrahasis Epic*. The truth of a myth, however, does not depend upon whether the events it relates are historical facts. The truth lies, rather, in the degree of wisdom and insight expressed by its basic views regarding humanity, the universe, and the gods. The same criterion of truth should be applied to the mythological materials which are found in the Bible. To ask whether there is more truth in the biblical myths is not to ask whether they are closer to the way things actually happened. Rather, what we should ask is whether the concepts of humanity, its place in the universe and its relation to God, as found in the Bible, are closer to the truth than are the comparable concepts in Babylonian myth.

The majority of Christians and Jews will feel, almost instinctively, that indeed the concepts found in the Bible are closer to the truth. For example, there is no divine flesh and blood that has gone into our makeup. The divine element in us is of a more spiritual nature as symbolized by the breath of Yahweh which brough life to the first man (Gen 2:7). God did not *need* human beings to till the soil for him. In fact, the garden was planted by God only *after* the creation of the first man and was obviously for the man's benefit, not for God's. And, finally, God is not so arbitrary and capricious that he would destroy the human race because they made too much noise and kept him from sleeping. If there was a flood (and biblical authors naively believed that such had indeed been the case), it was due to the sinfulness of the human race rather than the injustice of God.

This last point, the question of the flood and the justice of God, points out some of the limitations of myth. A single story can only say so much, and though it might express part of the truth, it might be incomplete. The biblical story of the flood has the advantage of preserving a concept of the justice of God. But the expression of this truth was paid for heavily by laying a tremendous burden of guilt upon the human race. The Babylonian story suffers from a picture of the gods which seems unworthy to us. On the other hand, the Babylonian version of the flood presents a view of humanity which is more balanced in its outlook. When persons are killed by natural disasters, it is not necessarily because they are thoroughly sinful and guilty, thus deserving of destruction. The Babylonians realized that we live in a universe where there are many forces and powers greater than we are. These powers are usually beneficial to us and favorable to life. But sometimes they lash out with no apparent reason and bring suffering and destruction upon us. The *Atrahasis Epic* expresses the view that such disasters are not due to human guilt but to the very nature of life, which often appears unfair to us.

In any case, our purpose in this section was to demonstrate that myth expresses some very fundamental religious ideas. While some myths may be closer to the truth than are others, we must be sensitive to the possibility that a single story cannot tell the whole truth and that it can perhaps be complemented by the partial truth embedded in another myth.

The *Atrahasis Epic* is primarily a story about the flood. One might think that an understanding of this myth was relevant only for the study of the biblical flood story. Such, however, is not the case. By helping us to see how mythological stories work, how they embody and express a people's self-understanding, the *Atrahasis Epic* provides invaluable help in our attempts to grasp the significance of the Adam and Eve story of Gen 2-3.

The Myth of Adapa[4]

The myth of Adapa is pieced together from three fragments stemming from Ashurbanipal's library plus an older and better preserved tablet which, though written in Babylonian, was found in Egypt among the Amarna archives (fourteenth century B.C.).

The preserved portion of the myth is brief, but very interesting. Adapa, who is the representative man, if not the first man, was out fishing one day when he got angry and broke the wing of the south wind. The gods summoned him up to heaven to account for this presumptuous act. Before the journey to heaven, Adapa received some advice from the god Enki. Enki informed him that he would meet two gate-keepers at the entrance to heaven and that if he flattered these two gatekeepers he would win them over to his side and they would help him win a favorable decision from the gods. Enki then warned Adapa that the gods would try to have him eat the bread of death and the water of death but that he should refuse to partake of them. As Adapa arrives at the entrance of heaven he follows the good advice of Enki and wins over the cooperation of the gatekeepers. He is apparently pardoned by the great gods. But when they offer him bread and water, he refuses to accept them. This is most unfortunate, because as he later finds out, they were the bread of life and the water of life. Had he partaken, he and the whole human race would have been immortal. It is too bad, but he lost his chance. Because of Adapa, therefore, the human race has, since that time, been subject to disease and death.

Like the story of Gilgamesh losing the plant of rejuvenation to a serpent, we have another account of a lost chance for immortality. Both of these stories can be compared to the account of the Tree of Life in the Garden of Eden. If Adam and Eve had eaten of this tree, both they and their descendants would have been immortal. Unfortunately, they lost the chance both for themselves and for us.

Notes

1. The English translation of the entire text is found in J. Pritchard (ed.), *Ancient Near Eastern Texts,* 3d ed. (Princeton, N.J.: Princeton University Press, 1969) 72-97 or A. Heidel, *The Gilgamesh Epic and Old Testament Parallels,* 2d ed. (Chicago: University of Chicago Press, 1949). An interesting and insightful discussion of the epic is found in T. Jacobsen, *The Treasures of Darkness* (New Haven: Yale University Press, 1976) 195-219.

2. For a more detailed comparison, see E. Fisher, *"Gilgamesh* and Genesis: The Flood Story in Context," *Catholic Biblical Quarterly* 32 (1970) 392-403.

3. For the text, see W.G. Lambert and A.R. Millard, *Atrahasis: The Babylonian Story of the Flood* (Oxford: Clarendon Press, 1969). There is a review of the Lambert and Millard volume by W.L. Moran in *Biblica* 51 (1970) 51-61. Moran also published "The Creation of Man in Atrahasis I," 192-248, *Bulletin of the American Schools of Oriental Research* 200 (1970) 48-56. See also T. Frymer-Kensky, "The Atrahasis Epic and Its Significance for Our Understanding of Genesis 1-9," *Biblical Archaeologist* 40 (1977) 147-154.

4. The text may be found in J. Pritchard, ed., *Ancient Near Eastern Texts,* 3d ed. (Princeton: Princeton University Press, 1969) 101-103 or in A. Heidel, *The Babylonian Genesis,* 2d ed. (Chicago: University of Chicago Press, 1951) 147-153.

Chapter Three

The Theology of the *J* Author

We have seen that the Adam and Eve story of Gen 2:4b-3:24 belongs to the *J* source of the Pentateuch. In order to understand this story, therefore, it will be helpful to get a broader picture of the work of the *J* author and the theological views which it contains, especially in that part of his work which is called the Primeval History.

In Chapter One we detailed the division of Gen 1-11 into *J* and *P* components. At this point we wish to focus in on the *J* *narrative* material. This means that we will put aside all the *P* material, all the genealogical information, even if it is *J*, and the story of Gen 6:1-4 which does not seem to belong to *J* in spite of the fact that it uses the divine name Yahweh. This leaves us with the five narrative units belonging to the *J* Primeval History:

1. Adam and Eve (Gen 2:4b–3:24)
2. Cain and Abel (Gen 4:1–26)
3. The Flood (Gen 6:4–8:22, in combination with *P*)
4. Noah and His Sons (Gen 9:18–27)
5. The Tower of Babel (Gen 11:1–9)

Sources Used by *J*

In general, it is clear that the *J* author drew upon a variety of legendary and mythological tales which were in circulation

51

in the ancient world. The way in which the biblical authors took over these pre-existing stories is clearest in the case of the flood story which is so similar to the Babylonian flood story that the connection is transparent. Of course we cannot be sure if the *J* author knew exactly the version of the flood which is preserved in the *Gilgamesh Epic* or in *Atrahasis*. It was, in any case, quite close.

For the rest of the Primeval History, we cannot be as certain regarding the origins of the material. The story of Adam and Eve has some striking parallels with the story of the "initiation and fall" of Enkidu, as well as with other elements of the *Gilgamesh Epic.*[1] On the other hand, both the Adam and Eve story and the Adapa Myth explain our mortality by the fact that ancestors failed to eat a substance which would have made them, and consequently us, immortal. Thus, while we do not have an exact Babylonian prototype or model for the Adam and Eve story, we can see that it belongs to a *type* of myth which was evidently popular in the ancient world.

On the other hand, the Cain and Abel story of Gen 4:1-26 reflects the ancient literary theme of the conflict between the farmer and the shepherd. In addition, the information given about Cain should probably be interpreted in the light of the ancient practice of telling stories about an ancestor who had the same name as the people descended from him. For Cain (Hebrew *Qyn*) is ancestor of the Kenite (Hebrew *Qyny*) tribe, just as Israel is ancestor of the Israelites. Stories such as this, while allegedly talking about an ancestor, were really intended to portray the character traits of the people supposedly descended from him. Perhaps, therefore, the description of Cain as someone with a special kind of mark, who as a wanderer, and who practiced sevenfold vengeance for bloodshed is based upon the observation of an historical group of people, the Kenites, whose existence is known from other biblical passages.

The connection between an historical people and the ancestor from whom they received their name is also an aspect of the story of Noah and his sons (Gen 9:18-27). In that account, the impious act of Ham, the father of the Canaanites, was certainly intended as a depiction of the immorality of the Canaanites.

Finally, the Tower of Babel story (Gen 11:1-9) was made possible by the existence of temple towers in many of the cities of Mesopotamia. The tall structures were intended by their builders as a way of honoring the various gods. To outsiders, however, they seemed to represent an arrogant attempt on the part of human beings to scale the heavens. One aspect of the story, on the other hand, is simply due to a play on words: Babel (a form of the city name Babylon) was the place where people began to babble.

Though much remains uncertain, the above summary will give at least a rough idea of where the J author got his source material. We will now go on to see what he did with this raw material and what he was tyring to say with it.

The Structure of J's Primeval History

If we look at the five main narrative blocks outlined above a certain symmetry can be pointed out. To begin with, the middle element, the flood story, differs from the four other stories. The first two and the last two stories are stories of sin and punishment. The flood story, however, does not mention a specific sin. The flood account also stands out in that it is the only instance where the death penalty is applied. In fact, it will be argued below, the flood story has a special function within the sequence of five narratives.

If we look at the specific sins in stories, 1, 2, 4, and 5, we find that in the first and last the sin committed is a direct offense against God while in stories 2 and 4 it is an offense against a fellow human being (a brother in #2, a father in #4). It seems, then that the following symmetrical pattern lies behind J's structure.

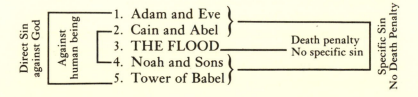

The Results of Sin

When we look at the results of sin in the four stories of the framework outlined above, we find an impressive list of the troubles which afflict us as human beings. In each case, there arises a situation which restricts the possibility for the full expansion and development of our human potential. Let us review these life-limiting phenomena.

In the Adam and Eve story we find a series of alienations. Man is alienated from the ground: Adam who came from the soil (Hebrew ʾădāmāh) should be in harmony with it, but instead there is conflict. The woman experiences conflict within herself, for her sexual desire draws her to a man who then reduces her to subjugation, perverting the equality between the sexes originally intended according to Genesis 2. The woman also experiences division within herself in that her role as mother will entail pain. And, finally, the original harmony of nature is ended and alienation and conflict will now characterize human beings and the world of the animals (represented by the serpent).

In the Cain and Abel story, we read that as a result of one murder, violence and bloodshed will spread geometrically: there will be sevenfold revenge for Cain, and seventy-sevenfold revenge for his descendant Lamech.

As a result of the sin committed by Noah's son, one nation will be subject to others. In modern terms, we call this imperialism.

Finally, in the Tower of Babel story we read of the complete breakdown of communication so that it is no longer even possible for people to talk to one another anymore.

According to the *J* author, all of these evils came into the world because of sin. We begin to see why *J* has selected these stories from the wealth of myth and legend undoubtedly available to him. He was claiming that our problems as human beings are due to sin. Moreover, he skillfully selected his materials in order to illustrate in a panoramic way the scope of the limiting results of that sin. We cannot help but admire the thoroughness with which he has depicted "the human problem."

The Function of the Flood Story

The above discussion does not yet say anything about the function of the flood story. We have already pointed out that it differs from the other four stories in that it does not involve a specific sin and that it is the only instance where the death penalty is applied. There is another peculiarity of the *J* flood story. At the beginning of the story, we are told that "Yahweh saw that the wickedness of humankind on earth was great and that the inclination of the thoughts of their hearts was evil continually" (Gen 6:5), so he decided to destroy the human race by the flood. Then at the end of the flood we read that God will never again destroy the human race by a flood because "the inclination of the hearts of humankind was evil since their youth" (Gen 8:21). The same phenomenon, namely the evil inclination of human hearts, leads God first to one decision, then to its opposite! A major point of the flood story, then, is to insist that humankind deserves the death penalty, but that God has decided not to execute this verdict. The *J* author apparently believed that in the four other narratives of the Primeval History the death penalty was called for (it is clearly pointed to in the Adam and Eve story and in the Cain and Abel story). Paradoxially, then, the function of the flood story is to speak of God's mercy by insisting that the sins of humankind deserve death.

If it seems at this point that the *J* author had a rather pessimistic view of human nature, it must be pointed out that such a negative attitude was bearable because he also believed, as we shall shortly see, that God has provided a solution for the human problem.

The Pivotal Function of Gen 12:1-4a

It has been proposed by a number of scholars that the key to a full understanding of *J*'s Primeval History is found in Gen 12:1-4a, the *J* account of the promise to Abram (= Abraham):

Yahweh said to Abram, "Go, now, from your land, from all your relatives and from your immediate family, to the land which I will designate. I will make a great nation out of you, and I will bless you, and I will make you famous. You will become a blessing. I will bless whoever blesses you, but he who dishonors you I will curse. Through you, all the communities of the earth will obtain blessing." So Abram went as Yahweh had commanded him.

The relationship between this promise and the preceding stories becomes apparent when we notice several interesting phenomena. To begin with, the promise account marks the first time since creation that God takes the initiative in getting a new series of events under way. In the five narrative units outlined above, it was always the case that human beings made the first move: Adam and Eve ate the fruit of the tree; Cain killed Abel; Noah's son dishonored his father; the people of Babel started to build a tower. God entered the picture only in *reaction* to human initiative. In Gen 12:1, however, it is God who takes the initiative of revealing himself to Abram without any action on Abram's part which could have motivated God to step in.

Along with this new element of divine initiative, we find something new in human behavior. This is stated in extremely brief fashion, but is nonetheless of cardinal importance: "So Abram went as Yahweh had commanded him." This is the first instance of obedience to God in the *J* history. We begin to suspect that the *J* author intended to establish a contrast between the stories of primeval times and the history which began with Abram's call. This suspicion is reinforced when we examine *J*'s use of the theme of blessing.

We note, to begin with, that in the *P* materials of Genesis 1-11, the idea of blessing is one of the key themes which is repeated as refrain (Gen 1:22, 28; 2:3; 5:2; 9:1-7). This theme of blessing is reinforced by the insistence on the goodness of creation (Gen 1:4, 10, 18, 21, 25, 31) and the related theme of covenant (Gen 9:8-17). The positive emphasis of *P*'s primeval history is very different from *J*. In the latter, there is no mention of any blessing for creation. The only place where a word connected with blessing occurs is in Gen 9:26 which the New American Bible translates,

"Blessed be the LORD, the God of Shem." Note that it is *God* who is blessed, not a human being.[2] For the *J* author, then, the primeval history is far from being a time of blessing and goodness. It is, rather, the time of sin and the curses which are its punishment. In view of this, it is all the more remarkable that within the short space of the promise to Abram, there are *five* cases of a form of the words "to bless" and "blessing." The contrast between *J*'s primeval history and his account of the history beginning with Abram is precisely a contrast between the time without blessing and the time when blessing becomes a possibility.

An important theological conviction of the *J* author now emerges. He believed that we have a tendency to refuse to accept our status as creatures and instead we try to infringe upon the realm which belongs to God. We want to be *like God* (Gen 3:5), take action against the life of a brother (Gen 4:8), and assure our own well-being by our arrogant attempts to scale the heavenly heights (Gen 11:4). When we act in this way, we end up doing the opposite of what we intended. For we bring upon ourselves pain and alienation (Gen 3:14-19), the multiplication of violence (Gen 4:15, 24), the subjugation of others (Gen 9:25-27), and, finally, the breakdown of communication with our fellow human beings (Gen 11:7-9). When, on the other hand, we let God be God and obediently follow the divine initiative, blessing becomes a possibility (Gen 12:1-4a).

The theological insight which *J* attempted to communicate in this contrasting of the Primeval History with the history beginning with Abram's call need not be taken to mean that all persons before Abram were completely sinful and that good people only began to exist with Abram. Indeed, we know from our own experience that there is both good and evil within any human community or individual and within any given historical period. It is impossible to divide the human race into a purely good camp and a purely evil camp. The *J* author should rather be understood as *using* the stoies of primeval times in order to describe in paradigmatic fashion the negative possibilities which are an aspect of behavior throughout all of history. In these stories, then, we learn of an aspect of the human condition which is found within all of us. To that extent, these are stories *about us*, rather than stories about persons who would have lived a long time ago.

J's Support of the Kingship of David and Solomon

We have already seen that the call of Abram in Gen 12:1-4a is a pivotal passage for understanding the theological message of the *J* author. We now turn our attention to an additional feature of this passage which reveals a further aspect of the *J* theology. What is at issue here is the statement in Gen 12:2, "I will make a great nation out of you." The reference to the "great nation" is peculiar to the *J version* of the promises made to the fathers. Apart from *J*, no other biblical author mentions it. We may therefore take the link with the "great nation" as *J*'s own contribution to the understanding of the promises made to the patriarchs. By means of this innovation, *J* gave a new interpretation to the promise tradition.

The Hebrew expression in question is *gôy gādôl*. These words do not refer simply to a numerically large group, but to a "great nation" in the political sense. Now we know that there was only one period in the history of Israel when it was (politically) a great nation; that was in the time of David and Solomon, precisely the time in which the *J* work was composed. In *J*'s view then, when God called Abram, God already had in mind the Davidic-Solomonic Empire. The latter, in a sense, was the goal toward which God was working right from the start. Therefore, the great nation of David and Solomon could be viewed as the *fulfillment* of the promise made to Abram. It is important to realize the magnitude of *J*'s innovation in reinterpreting the promise tradition in such a fashion. Before *J*'s work, the common understanding had been that the promises made to the patriarchs had been fulfilled in the time of Joshua when the descendants of the people who had escaped slavery in Egypt under the leadership of Moses had invaded the land of Canaan and settled in the "promised land." The new interpretation of *J* seems all the more striking when we realize that many of *J*'s contemporaries viewed the Davidic royal establishment as a betrayal of the ancient traditions of Israel. *J* gave theological legitimacy to the Empire by referring to it in his account of the promise. In view of this, a number of recent scholars have described *J*'s work as a piece of theologico-political propaganda in favor of the monarchy. This view has much in its favor, but it must be nuanced in the light of other evidence which shows that *J*'s support of the Davidic-Solomonic regime had important conditions and limits attached to it. Before getting to this subject, however, it is necessary to return briefly to the theme of blessing.

All the Communities of the Earth

In *J*'s account of the promise, there is a statement that "Through you, all the communities of the earth will obtain blessing" (Gen 12:3). The form of the verb "to bless" which occurs in the Hebrew text is transcribed *nibrĕkû*. The exact meaning of this verb form is debated. The rendering given above agrees with a number of modern translations, including the New American Bible, in giving it a universalistic interpretation. That is, the blessing is not understood to be limited to Abram and his descendants, but will, in some way, reach "all the communities of the earth." Some other translations have presented a different interpretation which is more restrictive. In this second view, the passage would only mean that Abram and his blessing will become so famous that when other communities of the earth pray for blessing, they will do so by wishing that they were as blessed as Abram. That is, Abram would become the *standard of blessing* without implying that other people will actually share the blessing which belongs to Abram and his descendants.

From the point of view of grammar, either interpretation is possible. Those who choose the more restrictive interpretation do so in part because they find it hard to believe that an author in the time of *J* would have been broad-minded enough to have such an enlightened universalistic perspective. This objection to the universalistic interpretation is not convincing, however. In fact, when we reflect upon the political situation at the time of the *J* author, we see that attention to the other nations was unavoidable. During the period of judges, Israel had been a simple agricultural society organized as a federation of twelve tribes. The relationship between Yahweh and Israel was simple. He was *their* God and they were *his* people. The other nations had their own gods and did not have any direct relationship with Yahweh (see, for example, Deut 32:8-9). That situation changed almost overnight as a result of David's conquests. Israel became the head of a moderate-sized empire. That complicated the old theological understanding. How, in this radically altered situation, was the relationship between Yahweh and the other nations conquered by David to be understood? The view which emerged was that Yahweh had a direct relationship with Israel and its king. But Yahweh now had a new (indirect) relationship with the nations that had been conquered by David or otherwise entered into treaty relations with him. It is through this religious understanding of the political situation that the idea could naturally develop that the blessings promised to the descendants of Abraham could overflow onto the other nations who would thus have a share in these blessings. This is not to say that the other communities were on an equal footing with Israel. They only shared in the blessings in a secondary and indirect fashion. In view of all this, the objection against the universalistic interpretation of *nibrĕkû* may be dismissed. Just as, in his Primeval History, *J* had depicted the problems faced by *all* humanity, not just by Israel, so too when he presents God's *solution* to these problems, it is a solution which concerns all humanity.

The Limits of Royal Power

The theological position of *J*, then, is that when the man who receives the promise, made by God's initiative, is willing to follow obediently, the great nation will arise and blessing will come (indirectly) to all the communities of the earth. Once again we detect strong support for the empire of David and Solomon. But exactly how is this all to work out? H.W. Wolff, in an important article on this subject, has argued convincingly that *J* illustrated the process in the way he reported the dealings of the patriarchs with foreigners.[3] When the patriarchs behave in a trusting and faithful manner, they do indeed bring blessings to others. See, for example, how Abraham's generosity ends by bringing prosperity to Lot in Genesis 13 and how Isaac's covenant with Abimelech in Genesis 26 brings peace (*shālôm*) to the Philistines. More important for our purposes, however, is the correlative point that when the patriarch fails to trust Yahweh and fails to act appropriately, he brings *trouble* to others rather than blessing! A good example is in Genesis 12, immediately after the promise account, where we read of Abram's going to Egypt with his wife. He is afraid that he will be killed and in order to save his own life he tells a lie and allows his wife to become involved in a compromising situation. This was due to lack of faith in Yahweh's intention to fulfill the promise. Abram attempted to safeguard the promise himself by taking the initiative back into his own hands. The result was disaster for the Egyptians (Gen 12:17). Other *J* version stories about the patriarchs make the same point. We see, therefore, that the blessing for all the families of the earth is not something automatic. It comes about only if the man who received or inherited the promise is willing to trust and to act in a faithful manner. The same must apply to the king who heads the "great nation." That king has the assurance of *J* that his royal power is part of Yahweh's plan. But the *J* author indirectly warns the king that the realization of blessing requires continued fidelity. Otherwise, he will fail in achieving the purpose of his vocation and will bring the curse upon all the communities of the earth. So we can see that *J*'s endorsement of the Davidic-Solomonic establishment includes a crucial conditional factor.

The limit which *J* places upon his support of the monarchy is also apparent in the Adam and Eve story of Genesis 2-3. There are many indications that the point of that story was intended to apply especially to the king. The evidence for this view will be discussed later in Chapter Four. For now let it suffice to say that *J* insisted that when the king refuses to accept the limits which God has placed on his authority, that is, when the king wants to be *like God* and have universal power and control,

he brings disaster upon himself just as surely as Adam did. The
J author, then, is far from being a completely pro-establishment
spokesman.

Conclusion

We started out by seeing how the *J* author had borrowed
mythological and legendary materials about "primeval times."
We have seen, however, that he was not interested in just repeat-
ing the stories for the sake of satisfying our curiosity about the
early history of the human race. He transformed and structured
his source material in order to express his profound understanding of human nature and of our relationship to God. Moreover,
he boldly reinterpreted the religious traditions he had inherited
by seeing them within the light of the social and political reali-
ties in which he lived. In doing this he underscored the heavy
responsibility which comes with the vocation to political
leadership and the religious and ethical limits which must apply
to the use of power. The intellectual achievement of this author
is therefore a most impressive one. No wonder that modern
commentators have recognized him as the "first theologian" of
ancient Israel.

Notes

1. See the discussion in Chapters Two and Four.
2. The New American Bible follows the clear meaning of the Hebrew text at this point. The translators of the Revised Standard Version, on the other hand, believed there was a mistake in the Hebrew
and corrected the text to read, "Blessed by the LORD my God be
Shem." I believe the Revised Standard Version is in error here and that
its "correction" ends up obscuring the intent of the *J* author.
3. H.W. Wolff, "The Kerygma of the Yahwist," *Interpretation* 20
(1966) 131-158.

Chapter Four

The Story of Adam and Eve: A History of Meaning

We have examined a number of Babylonian myths and have analyzed the theology of the *J* author, especially as it is reflected in his Primeval History. All of this was to serve as background for understanding the Adam and Eve story. The material studied in the earlier chapters of this book, in other words, provides aspects of the broader context which will help us get at the meaning of chapters 2 and 3 of Genesis.

To speak of "the meaning" of the Adam and Eve story, however, is misleading. We will see that a considerable number of different meanings can be found in the story. We become aware of these different meanings when we take an historical perspective on the material and its interpretation. Accordingly, we will look at a number of stages of meaning: the meaning of the material before it was used by the *J* author; the meaning it had for the *J* author; new meanings which were found in the story in the history of its interpretation; finally, the meaning or meanings the story can have for us today.

Before the Work of the *J* Author

It is clear from clues within the Adam and Eve story itself, as well as from reflection on the Babylonian texts surveyed in

Chapter Two, that the *J* author combined and adapted literary traditions which had been in existence long before his time. Unfortunately, however, there is no way we can be sure about which form those traditions had before he put them into the form we now find in Genesis 2:4b-3:24. In this section, therefore, we will admittedly by doing some guess work. It is hoped that the reader will agree that the guesses are reasonable ones.

It is by comparing the narrative of Genesis 2–3 with similar ancient Near Eastern texts that we can best form a general idea of the kind of source materials used by the *J* author and the earlier meaning of those materials. Our first observation is a negative one: so far, scholars have not been able to find an ancient text which would parallel all of the features of Gen 2–3. The latter, rather, seems to reflect a variety of mythological themes which were originally found in different sources. We will assume, for simplicity's sake, that it is the *J* author who combined these different themes into the story which we now have.[1]

Though the Enkidu story found in the *Gilgamesh Epic* does not parallel all of the elements in the Adam and Eve story, it is nonetheless the single most striking analogy. Both Adam and Enkidu are created from clay and placed in a life situation of harmony with the world of nature. Enkidu runs naked with gazelles and knows nothing of sexuality; Adam is naked in the presence of a woman, but, childlike, experiences no shame or embarassment. Adam and Enkidu are both "initiated" into a new form of life by a woman: Enkidu has intercourse with the temple prostitute; Adam takes and eats the fruit given him by Eve. Enkidu is told, after this initiation, "Wise art thou, O Enkidu, like a god art thou." Eve is told that as a result of eating the forbidden fruit, "your eyes will be opened; you will become like god(s) knowing good from bad." As a result, both Enkidu and Adam experience a "fall" from the blessed existence of childlike simplicity and become part of the "real world" of adults where responsibility, pain, and hardship must be endured, and ultimately the reality of death must be faced up to. Finally, there is an interesting similarity in that the prostitute clothes Enkidu before leading him away from his home in the steppe-land, whereas Yahweh makes leather garments for Adam and Eve as he drives them from the Garden of Eden.[2]

The parallels are so striking that we can unhesitatingly affirm that one of the sources used by the *J* author was a story analogous to the Enkidu narrative.[3] This does not mean it is precisely the Enkidu narrative which we know from the *Gilgamesh Epic* that served as a model for *J*. There must have been a considerable number of different versions of this story circulating in the ancient world. However, the comparison does give us a rough idea of the kind of prototype *J* might have been working with. More specifically, the comparison suggests that sexual experience might have been more prominent in the pre-*J* form of the tradition. In the Enkidu account, the initiation is specifically sexual in nature. This raises the possibility that the forbidden fruit from the tree of "knowledge of good and bad" originally symbolized sexual experience. In fact, the verb "to know" which is used at this point occurs frequently in the Hebrew Bible in reference to sexual intercourse (compare "carnal knowledge"). Moreover, there are a number of aspects of Genesis 2–3 which involve sexual imagery. Before the forbidden experience, for example, the man and woman are naked but not ashamed. That is, they are like little children who are not aware of their sexuality. After the experience, however, they have found out something they didn't know before, and they feel that they must cover their bodies. Sexual symbolism may also be intended by the presence of the serpent which occurs as a phallic symbol in the ancient Near East as elsewhere in the world. Finally, we note that the punishments which come upon the woman relate to her sexual desire and to her role as a mother (Gen 3:16). While the punishments imposed upon the man are not as directly sexual, they do involve the adult male role of bread-winner—a role which a young man assumes at the time of sexual maturity.

It is not unlikely, therefore, that in an earlier form the Adam and Eve story dealt with the transformation which all human beings undergo when they become experienced in sexual matters, leaving childhood behind and entering into adulthood. It is very important to emphasize, however, that in this earlier stage of the myth, the experience of initiation was *not* viewed as a sin. Our guide here must be the Enkidu story where no moral judgment is placed upon Enkidu's lying with the prostitute. It is something normal and necessary, an event which has beneficial consequences, although unfortunately it also entails undesirable results. When the *J* author took over the story, he made of it a story of sin and its consequences, a story which was part of a sequence of episodes making up his Primeval History as examined in Chapter Three. The introduction of sin and guilt into the story of the initiation of the primeval man follows the pattern which is evident in *J*'s handling of the flood story. As we have seen, the Babylonian prototype of the Deluge account does not blame the flood on human sinfulness, but on the arbitrary behavior of (some of) the gods. So the injection of human sin into earlier stories which did not deal with this topic can be seen as typical of *J*'s procedure. This, however, is not the only way in which *J* modified the story. For it seems that *J* no longer understood the act symbolized by eating the fruit of the tree of knowledge as sexual initiation. This is seen in Gen 2:23-24 where sexuality is affirmed, in a positive light, before the temptation scene.

To summarize the above discussion, we see that in the pre-*J* form of the story, the act of initiation probably consisted in sexual experience but was not viewed as sinful. In the *J* form of the story the act involved is a sin which results in an unequivocal "fall," but that act is no longer identified with introduction to sexual experience. The aberrant Christian traditions which have identified sexual intercourse and "original sin" are thus seen to have confused aspects which are derived from two quite distinct stages in the handing on of these traditions.

Genesis 2-3 contains other themes in addition to those found in the Enkidu story. Notably there is the concept of a certain food, the eating of which results in the avoidance of death. This theme is found in the Adapa myth and in the *Gilgamesh Epic*. Both of these texts agree with Genesis 3 that something unfortunate happened which made it impossible for human beings to eat this marvelous food. As a result, death is our unavoidable fate. Yet another example is the idea that the human being is made of clay yet contains a divine element. This view is found in the *Atrahasis Epic* as well as in Genesis 2. In both places the human being was created in order to do agricultural work. In *Atrahasis* this work is for the benefit of the gods, whereas the biblical God is not dependent upon the work of the creature but instead plants the garden for the benefit of the human being.

There are other less important thematic elements in the story which must antedate the work of *J*. What has been listed above, however, is sufficient to give us a general idea of the range of meaning expressed by the materials of Gen 2-3 before they were given the form which we now have.

The Meaning Intended by the *J* Author

A Basic View. What meaning did the *J* author intend to convey by the retelling of the Adam and Eve story in his own particular way? A general answer to this question was already given in Chapter Three where we examined the whole of the *J* author's Primeval History. From that perspective, the story presents a typical expression of the human problem: we want to act independently of God, on our own initiative, and in so doing we bring upon ourselves all manner of trouble which limits the potential for a full life. The antithesis of Adam and Eve is Abram who "went, as Yahweh had commanded him." When we look at the counter-example of Abram in this way, then the essential nature of Adam and Eve's sin is quite simple: it is disobedience.

It needs to be pointed out that the modern understanding of obedience is not the same as that which was held by ancient people, including the *J* author. We have a conviction that truly human choice and behavior are characterized by freedom. They flow from a source deep within a person and are in harmony with all the individual features which makes each one of us who he or she is. As a result, demands for obedience which come from a source outside of the individual are perceived as limiting and oppressive, even if the command comes from God.[4] Insofar as we share this modern attitude, we are not likely to be comfortable with the *J* author's view that obedience is the key virtue and that the prototypical sin is disobedience. The ancient author, however, lived in a culture which placed a high value on obedience to parents, elders, and political leaders. In such a culture, the need to obey would not even be questioned and would certainly not be considered as lessening human freedom and dignity. We do not have to be in full agreement with these cultural presuppositions, but we do need to recognize their presence in the biblical material.

It is possible that disobedience, pure and simple, is all that the *J* author saw in the action of Adam and Eve. If so, then the "knowledge of good and bad" would likewise have a simple meaning: they knew what was good as long as they obeyed, but by disobeying they experienced what was bad along with its consequences. The majority of scholars, however, think there is more to it and that the extraordinarily rich symbolism of the story was intended to say much more about who we are as human beings, how we make choices, how pain enters into our lives, and how we relate to God. Though they agree that there is more to it than just disobedience, however, scholars are far from agreeing on exactly what it is that the *J* author intended to convey in his formulation of the story.

The purpose of this chapter is to review the various meanings of the story, and the present section of the chapter aims at the meaning intended by the *J* author. But we find that the experts can't agree on exactly what that is! This can be extremely frustrating, especially to the average reader who expects the experts to be able to provide some answers. In Chapter Five we will return to this lack of consensus among the experts. For now, I will make a few general observations which a majority of exegetes would probably agree with. This will at least steer the reader in the right direction.

"*You will become like gods, knowing good and bad.*" The principal key to understanding the specific nature of the sin of Adam and Eve must lie in these words, spoken by the serpent. There are many different theories as to how the statement is to be understood. Nonetheless, it is possible to make some observations which would be widely accepted, even by writers who disagree on specific details.

It is helpful, first of all, to be aware that the Hebrew word "to know" (*yāda*) has a broader range of meaning than its English counterpart. The word is by no means limited to intellectual comprehension but sometimes means "to experience." The best illustration of how this goes beyond the activity of the mind is the frequent use of the word to refer to sexual intercourse, for example in Gen 4:1, "The man knew Eve, his wife, and she conceived, etc." Other uses of the verb have the meanings "to care about, be concerned about someone or something." In such cases there is a dynamic impulse toward activity which clearly moves beyond mere mental activity.

As to the expression "good and bad" we can begin with the negative observation that it refers neither to abstract philosophical categories nor to moral/ethical value judgments. Rather, "good" refers to that which is beneficial, profitable and useful, whereas "bad" is that which is harmful or injurious. This practical or functional range of meaning is echoed by the woman's observation that the tree was desirable "for becoming wise." The verb "to be wise" (*haśkîl*) also means "to be successful." These observations fit in with what was said about the verb "to know" extending to experience and activity. To know good and bad, therefore, means possession of the means of being successful in the management of one's existence. The saying that "knowledge is power" is applicable here in a manner which transcends the meaning usually intended by the saying in English.

Another aspect of the expression "good and bad" deserves to be pointed out. Biblical Hebrew often uses phrases which mention two extremes as a way of designating a totality. This is like saying "from soup to nuts," or "from A to Z," where everything in between is also included. This connotation of the expression is not necessarily incompatible with what was said about the functional overtones of "good and bad." Putting these observations together might suggest that "knowing good and bad" means a universal knowledge leading to universal power. It becomes apparent then why the desire to achieve this kind of "knowledge" is tantamount to striving to become "like god(s)." The attempt of human beings to achieve the divine prerogatives of omniscience and omnipotence means that they want to go beyond the limits which are inherent to their status as creatures. They are trying to obtain for themselves something which belongs only to God and thus to usurp the place of God.

"*They knew they were naked.*" The immediate and concrete result of eating from the forbidden tree is that "the eyes of both of them were opened and they knew they were naked. So they sewed together fig leaves and made themselves loincloths." This contrasts with the earlier statement that "though the two of them were naked, the man and his wife, they were not ashamed." Though some modern readers of more liberal inclination might think that the natural acceptance of nudity before the fall was in every way preferable to the (culturally conditioned and unnatural?) shame which was experienced after the fall, there can be no doubt that the *J* author shared the thinking of ancient Israel that it is *right* for us to cover our bodies. This means that something *positive* has resulted from the act of Adam and Eve. They have correctly understood something they had not "known" before and went on to use their creative abilities to make clothing for themselves. They are thus like God who in Gen 2:18 understood that "it is not good for the man to be alone," and went on to do something about it. Unfortunately, this positive development is only one side of the coin. The other side is that their efforts to solve their problem are not fully successful (see Gen 3:21). Indeed they *fear* God's presence and must hide themselves from him. This separation or alienation of the man and woman from God is only the beginning, for in the punishments decreed by God, alienation from the earth and the world of the animals makes its appearance. The relation between the man and the woman is disturbed and she experiences inner alienation in that her highest powers become a source of suffering. The serpent had not lied. They did acquire new, godlike status (see Gen 3:4-5). Unfortunately, the baneful consequences of their act more than outweigh this gain.

In conclusion, we may observe that the *J* author probably meant to express more than simple disobedience in this story. The prototypical human failing is a refusal to accept the limits intrinsic to being a creature. The attempt to gain universal knowledge and power is an arrogant and mistaken attempt to become god-like by usurping something which belongs to the creator. There is a sense in which the effort succeeds, and that's what makes it so "tempting." Ultimately, however, the attempt to be *more* than human leads to a condition which is less than human. By trying to go *beyond the limits* we lose the chance to achieve that measure of fulfillment which is proper to the limited existence we have as created persons.

Some Possible Refinements. What has been said so far might not receive the full agreement of all Old Testament scholars, but the great majority would be in general agreement with the substance of what I have written. However, many of them would want to give a somewhat different emphasis or to push the interpretation further along lines which give a more specific definition to the story. Two issues which arise in this connection will be discussed briefly because of their importance. I am referring to the possibility that the *J* author intended to attack the Canaanite fertility rites or to comment on the abuse of royal power.

Polemic against Canaanite Religion. A considerable number of scholars have argued that the sin symbolized by the tree of knowledge is participation in the religious rituals of the Canaanites, rituals which were especially concerned with sexuality and fertility. These scholars stress the sexual overtones of the Adam and Eve story, summarized above, but claim that the references are to *ritual* sexual practices which are known from Canaanite written documents as well as the preachments of the prophets. They remind us that the serpent is a prominent figure in Canaanite religious texts and art. Moreover, pointing to the parallel between the serpent's statement about becoming "like god(s), knowing good and bad" and the statement in the *Gilgamesh Epic,* "Wise art thou, O Enkidu, like a god art thou," they stress that the latter statement was made precisely by a *cultic prostitute,* that is, an official participant in the fertility religion. Thus the benefits promised by the serpent (symbolizing Canaanite religion) would be precisely those promised by the fertility cult. The prototypical sin condemned in the Adam and Eve story, therefore, would be the same as the fundamental sin opposed by prophets such as Elijah and Hosea, namely, the abandonment of Yahweh in order to become involved in Canaanite practices.[5]

This hypothesis is a very attractive one, though the evidence is not conclusive. And there are some objections. For example, there is no other evidence that opposition to Canaanite religion was a major theological concern at the time of the *J* author.[6] Moreover, the statement that "the serpent was the most clever of all the animals created by Yahweh," in Gen 3:1, combined with the details of the curse of the serpent in 3:14-15, gives the impression that the text is speaking of a real snake, not about a symbol of magical powers or of the Canaanite fertility religion. Nonetheless, it must be admitted that the interpretation of the Adam and Eve story as a polemic against Canaanite religion is more widely accepted by scholars than the view which will be discussed next.

Adam as King. It would probably never enter into the mind of the average reader to think that Adam symbolizes the king. However, the possibility is not as far-fetched as might first appear. The clearest piece of evidence in this connection is the passage Ezekiel 28:11-19 where the prophet is attacking the king of Tyre. In this prophetic condemnation the king is compared to the man who was placed in the Garden of Eden at his creation. He dwelled there in innocence until he was found guilty of evil and was driven out. It is generally recognized by Old Testament scholars that this passage alludes to a variation of the Garden of Eden story. The version referred to by Ezekiel differs from the version in Gen 2-3 in a number of respects. Most important is the fact that in Ezekiel, it is presumed that the man in the garden was a king!

If we had just the Genesis and Ezekiel passages to go by, it could be argued that the connection with the king was an innovation attributable to Ezekiel. However, a number of lines of evidence suggest that the identification of the man in the garden with a king was standard. For example, a study of the theme of the tree of life in the ancient world shows that it is a king who is the gardener in charge of guarding this tree. Also, we have already seen that the plant of rejuvenation snatched away by a snake was connected with Gilgamesh, king of Uruk, according to Babylonian lore. The theme of the first man as king may be reflected in other Old Testament passages. For example, Psalm 8, which asks "What is man that you should be mindful of him?" and speaks of him as a little less than the gods, *crowned* with glory and honor, and *ruling* over the works of God, is probably based upon traditions which spoke of the first human being as king.

In view of the above observations, it is quite possible that when the ancient heard or read the story of Adam and Eve he would naturally presume that it was a story about a king since that was simply the way the story was always told. Although this cannot be called a majority view, still there are many exegetes who hold that the *J* author intended his story to be understood as referring to the king. This hypothesis can be held in combination with a number of other interpretations discussed above. For example, Adam's identity as king would fit nicely with the view that the story of the fall is a polemic against the Canaanite fertility rites since the principal actor in the latter was precisely the king. Alternately, one might promote, as suggested above, the view that the desire to "know good and bad" is an effort to achieve unlimited power. In this case, the Adam and Eve story could be understood as a warning to the reigning king that if he tried to grasp for power beyond the limits imposed by Yahweh, he would bring trouble upon himself and his people. This view has been attractively presented by Walter Brueggemann and was followed in Chapter Three in my overview of theology of the *J* author.[7]

After the *J* Author

We have seen that old mythological traditions which had meaning in their own right were given new meaning by the *J* author when he reworked them to suit his own particular theological purposes. The process did not end with the *J* author, however, for the need of successive generations to interpret the text led them to find new meanings which were as much of an innovation in comparison to the *J* author as his own creation

was in respect to his predecessors. This is a very important phenomenon for us to recognize, for as we see how our ancient fore-
bears found their own meaning in the traditional text, we too
may be encouraged to accept the responsibility to work out our
own interpretation. The history of the interpretation of Genesis
2-3 is a particularly rich one. We will not attempt a comprehen-
sive survey, but will select a few aspects that will serve to illustrate the general process. The examples chosen all involve
important areas of contemporary theological reflection in their
own right.

Original Sin. In the traditional formulation of the doctrine
of original sin, it is usually understood that the sinful act of
Adam and Eve had a twofold result for all their descendants.
First, the blissful existence of paradise along with its preternatu-
ral gifts was lost to all members of the human race. Second, the
guilt for this sin was inherited by all their descendants who thus
stood in need of salvation. The term "original sin" is used to describe the state or condition of sin into which all persons are
born as well as the act of the first couple which was the cause of
that state or condition.

It can be seen that this doctrine goes considerably beyond
the meaning intended by the *J* author. When we look at the
whole series of stories of which the Primeval History is composed (above, Chapter Three) it becomes apparent that each suc-
ceeding generation was fully capable of sinning on its own
without needing to inherit any guilt from Adam and Eve. In
fact, when we studied this series of stories, we saw that all of
them, including the Adam and Eve episode, provide prototypes
or paradigms of the ways in which we act as human beings.
They are important, not as events which happened once in the
past, but as models of what keeps happening over and over again
in each of our lives. The idea of a sin which took place in the
beginning, the guilt for which was passed on from generation to
generation, is a later development. The concept can be found in
a non-biblical Jewish work which was probably written during
the first century A. D. and which is called Fourth Esdras. We
read in chapter 7, verse 118 of this work, "O thou Adam, what
hast thou done! For though it was thou that sinned, the fall was

not thine alone, but ours also who are thy descendants!" This text demonstrates that the concept of an original sin passed on to the descendants of Adam was known to Jewish thinkers during the period in which Christianity was developing. The idea was used by St. Paul who spoke of the contrast between Adam and Christ. Through Adam, sin and death entered the world and affected the whole human race. But now through one man, Christ, who is the new Adam, grace becomes a possibility for the whole human race. This contrast, found in chapter 5 of the Epistle to the Romans, may therefore be regarded as a way of speaking about the universality of the salvation revealed in the life, death, and resurrection of Christ. These theological concepts of St. Paul were more fully elaborated by St. Augustine whose teaching on the matter of original sin came to be the generally accepted view within the Church.

It is quite striking that in contrast with Fourth Esdras and the New Testament, the Hebrew Bible does not contain a single reference back to the Genesis story of Adam and Eve. The idea of a state or condition of sin inherited by the descendants of Adam and Eve because of their sin appears to have been nonexistent for centuries after the time of the *J* author. Of course, the dominant theological understanding in Israel, including the *J* author himself, was fully convinced that human beings were sinful. But they did not view this sinfulness as the consequence of one action at the beginning of history.

While the doctrine of original sin was a late development of only peripheral interest in Jewish theology, it is frequently made quite central to the Christian proclamation. It is precisely the hopelessness of the sinful situation in which we are said to be born that establishes the need for the salvation which is experienced in Christ. Moreover, the universality of original sin can be balanced off against the universality of salvation: as all men sinned and were condemned in Adam, so all are saved in Christ. We see, therefore, that much of what the Christian tradition has said about original sin was actually a way of making statements about Christ. Now that biblical scholarship has made it apparent that the *J* author did not intend the meaning found in the story by later interpreters, theologians have suggested new ways of looking at the doctrine of original sin which preserve the Christological insights of the tradition while respecting the intention of the author of the Adam and Eve story. An up-to-date and very readable survey of these developments may be found in Zachary Hayes, *What Are They Saying About Creation?*[8]

Before leaving the topic of original sin, I would like to comment very briefly on a related matter. After Christian theologians began understanding the story of the fall as an account of the original sin which passed on to all descendants of Adam and Eve, they found in Gen 3:15 a hint of the eventual coming of a savior. That text, in its original meaning, simply announced that undying enmity would exist between human beings (descendants of the woman) and snakes. Christian theologians, however, took the serpent as symbolizing Satan and understood the Hebrew collective noun for descendants as a reference to one specific person. Since the serpent only attacks the *heel* of this person whereas the latter attacks the *head* of the serpent, this was taken to imply victory over the serpent. This suggestion of a future victory of a deliverer or savior over the serpent came to be called the *Protoevangelium*, a foreshadowing of the victory of Christ over Satan. We have here another example of reading more into the text than could possibly have been meant by the *J* author. The fact that the same Hebrew verb is used to describe what the serpent does to the head of the woman's offspring as is used for what the latter does to the serpent's head does not suggest that the author meant to say anything about the eventual victory of one party over the other.[9]

The Role of Women. In recent years we have become increasingly aware that many of our social institutions and much of our cultural heritage exhibit prejudicial tendencies unfavorable to women and leading to their oppression. It is not surprising that the Genesis stories are often discussed in this context. The story of Gen 2-3 is sometimes quoted by conservatives in order to support the subordination of women. The same account is frequently denounced by feminists who see in it an archetypical example of ideas which denigrate women and contribute to their oppression.

There are several aspects of Gen 2-3 which enter into the

discussion. First is the fact that in Gen 2 the creation seems to focus on the man, whereas the woman appears to come in at the end, almost as an afterthought, to be a "helper" to the man. Furthermore, the woman is made from the man's rib (a part of his anatomy which is apparently dispensable) suggesting that he has a kind of superiority, or at least priority over against the woman. Next comes the role of the woman in eating from the forbidden tree. Since the woman eats first and then gives it to the man, it has often been understood that she is here depicted as a *temptress* who brings evil into the world by seducing the man into sin. Finally, the statement in 3:16, "You shall have sexual desire for your husband, but he will act as your master," has been seen as scriptural justification for male domination.

If we are to deal with the Genesis stories in a way which is sensitive to issues related to women, our first task is to determine to what extent the anti-woman interpretations sketched above can be attributed to the intention of the *J* author and to what extent they are later interpretations that are out of harmony with the actual views of the original author.

I must confess that my strong admiration for the *J* author makes me tend to respond defensively when I hear him accused of sexism. So, for example, it can be argued that the order of creation is designed to give honor to the woman as the crown of creation and that the use of the man's rib only enhances her dignity since the animals and the man were made from mere clay. One can also insist, with the majority of modern commentators, that there is not any hint in the story that the woman *tempts* the man or that she is in any way more guilty than he is.[10] Finally, it can be claimed that according to the *J* author God's original plan was for the man and the woman to be equal and that such is what is meant by the expression "suitable companion" in Gen 2:19, as most modern scholars agree. The social fact of male supremacy which the *J* author could not help but observe in his world was viewed by him as a distortion of God's original intent, the result of bad human choices.

The approach which argues that the views prejudicial to women are not really found in the text is also taken by Phyllis Trible, a feminist theologian who is a recognized biblical scholar. In her stimulating and insightful treatment of Gen 2-3 she goes much further than what was suggested above.[11] Trible argues that the Hebrew word *'ādām* when used of the human creature before the appearance of the woman refers to a sexually undifferentiated being (not exactly the same as an *androgyne*) and that both sexes appear at the same time. The text, therefore, would not be affirming the superiority of the male. In comparing the role of the man and the woman in the eating of the forbidden fruit she finds that as the characters are described in the text, it is the woman who comes off better: "If the woman is intelligent, sensitive, and ingenious, the man is passive, brutish, and inept."[12]

Because of my admiration for the *J* author, I would like to be able to agree with Trible that the account in Gen 2-3 is free of sexist bias. However, I am not fully convinced by her arguments. In the final analysis, it seems to me, there remain at least some elements of male dominant, patriarchal, thinking in the narrative. A biblical exegesis sympathetic to the feminist cause need not deny the presence of patriarchal attitudes in the Bible. A more realistic route, in my opinion, is to recognize the sexist presuppositions where they occur but to insist that these are not binding upon us today but rather are aspects of the ancient world view which we can and must strive to transcend. In a sense, the narrative of Gen 2-3 invites us to do just that. The *J* author could not see, in his world, any possibility of changing the social fact of male domination. But he indicated that it was not part of God's original plan. What was impossible in the time of the Israelite kings, however, is now politically and sociologically feasible. There is nothing to suggest that the situation described in the narrative is one that we are morally bound to perpetuate. That is, the statements of Gen 3:14-19 are *descriptive*, not *prescriptive*. This is in fact the way in which the other punishments listed have always been understood. Modern farmers use herbicides and drive air conditioned tractors in spite of Gen 3:17-19. And not even fundamentalists have ever countered the ecological insight that snakes are beneficial by demanding, on the basis of Gen 3:15, that we step on every one we see. The *J* author took upon himself the task of explaining the origin of the subjugation of women. We can take as our task the creation of a society in which each human person is free.

Regarding the issues raised by contemporary feminist awareness, therefore, three points need to be made. First, the *J* author himself was not as sexist as he is made out to be by some feminists and by reactionary proponents of male supremacy. In fact, there is some evidence that his views were relatively enlightened for the time in which he lived. Second, it must be admitted that the *J* author was limited by the cultural perspective in which he lived and that he took for granted the male domination which prevailed in patriarchal society. Third, we are challenged to go beyond the *J* author and work toward the day when all traces of sexism will be eliminated.

Marriage and Divorce. According to the New Testament, Jesus once was involved in a debate with the Pharisees about divorce. As this debate is reported in Mt 19:3-9, Jesus refers to the saying of Gen 2:24, "For this reason a man shall leave his father and mother and be joined to his wife, and the two shall become one flesh." Jesus understands the verse as an argument against the legitimacy of divorce and says, "What therefore God has joined together, let not man put asunder." He concludes the discussion by saying, "Whoever divorces his wife, except for unchastity, and marries another, commits adultery."[13]

It does not appear likely that all of this was intended by the *J* author. The latter, after all, lived in a culture which accepted polygamy. In his stories of the patriarchs, he speaks of the several wives of the Israelite ancestors without giving any indication that he disapproved of the practice. Moreover, the whole of the ancient world at that time, including the Mosaic Law, recognized the legitimacy of divorce. If the *J* author had intended to express a startling new view of marriage and divorce, he would have needed to express his view much more clearly. The fact that the Old Testament tradition nowhere reflects such an understanding supports the conclusion that the position of Jesus was an innovation.

In all likelihood, the *J* author's statement about two becoming one flesh referred primarily to sexual union. The verse constitutes one of those aetiologies which are characteristic of the *J* author and which were discussed in Chapter One. These aetiologies provide folkloristic explanations for striking phenomena. In this case the powerful attraction between the sexes is explained by telling how the woman was created from a part taken from the man. Such aetiological explanations do not necessarily conceal profound insights. In Gen 3:14, for example, we are provided with an aetiology of why serpents crawl on their bellies and "eat dust." The inconsequentiality of this piece of information serves to warn us against reading too much into other aetiologies of the *J* work.

The New Testament passage which connects Gen 2:24 with the question of divorce, therefore, is a further example of a later interpretation finding in the text new meaning which was not intended by the original author. Such new interpretations need not be labeled "mistakes," for they can be valuable perceptions of a new truth which reveals itself to the interpreter through the text. This meaning can be *found* in the text, even though its author was not aware of its presence. The case of Jesus' interpretation of Gen 2:24 is especially informative in this regard. It reveals a more profound understanding of the personal communion possible in marriage than is expressed by the earlier biblical material. Moreover, it strikes a blow for justice by insisting to a society where men could easily divorce their wives (but not vice versa) that it was not legitimate for men to dismiss their wives except for the gravest of reasons.[14]

Conclusion

The story of Gen 2-3 underwent an ongoing process of interpretation as did other parts of the Bible. Later readers found in the texts meanings which could not have been meant by the original author. Sometimes this would result in positive development of theological understanding as in the New Testament reflections on marriage and divorce. In other cases, such as that of original sin, the new interpretation provided a vehicle for articulating very fundamental theological insights, but in a way that would pose problems for later generations of theologians and require them to work out new ways of expressing the central convictions of the tradition. Finally, there are some examples, such as the sexist interpretation of Gen 2-3, which have led to regrettable consequences that need to be repudiated. In any case, the productivity of earlier generations of interpreters impels us on to the task of finding new meaning for old stories within our own historical context.

Notes

1. It is possible that an earlier author, Israelite or non-Israelite, had already made some of the combinations and modifications before the work of *J*. It is also possible that some of the minor themes were inserted by later editors or redactors. These refinements are debated in the scholarly literature but need not occupy us in this book.

2. The idea of a plant, the eating of which makes death avoidable (*Gilgamesh Epic*, Tablet 11, lines 266-282; Genesis 2:9; 3:22), and the intervention of a serpent (*Gilgamesh Epic*, Tablet 11, lines 287-289, Gen 3:1ff.) are further parallels between the Adam and Eve story and the *Gilgamesh Epic*. Since they do not belong to the Enkidu episode, however, they are not as relevant in the present context.

3. See J.A. Bailey, "Initiation and the Primal Woman in Gilgamesh and Genesis 2-3," *Journal of Biblical Literature* 89 (1970) 137-150.

4. A system of ethics in which the law (Greek *nomos*) governing human behavior is thought to come from a source which is other (Greek *heteros*) than the inner nature of the human person may be labeled "heteronomous." Theologians debate whether or not a theology of obedience needs to be understood as heteronomous. Of course more conservative theologians may find that a heteronomous system is nothing to apologize for but is, for them, precisely the advantage of Christian behavior: the human is transcended by surrendering the will to God.

5. A classical presentation of this view may be found in J.L. McKenzie, *The Two-Edged Sword* (Garden City, N.Y.: Image Books, 1966) 113-125.

6. The history of the Yahwistic opposition to the worship of the Canaanite fertility god Baal is discussed in my book *Rank Among the Canaanite Gods: El, Baal and the Rephaim.* "Harvard Semitic Monographs" 21 (Missoula, Mt.: Scholars Press, 1979) 59-67.

7. See W. Brueggemann, "David and His Theologian," *Catholic Biblical Quarterly* 30 (1968) 156-181.

8. Zachary Hayes, O.F.M. *What Are They Saying About Creation?* (New York: Paulist Press, 1980) especially 68-92. Hayes also discusses how theology can come to terms with modern scientific explanations of the origins of the physical universe and of the human race in terms of evolution.

9. For a fuller discussion of this topic see B. Vawter, *On Genesis: A New Reading* (Garden City, N.Y.: Doubleday, 1977) 82-84.

10. This does not explain why the author presents the *woman* as the one who has the dialogue with the serpent and eats first. Perhaps this was just the way the story was told in the traditions which served as sources for the *J* author and he has followed the tradition without intending to convey any specific point thereby.

11. P. Trible, *God and the Rhetoric of Sexuality* (Philadelphia: Fortress Press, 1978) 72-143.

12. *Ibid.*, 113.

13. The New Testament quotations are taken from the New American Bible.

14. New Testament scholars are not agreed as to what is meant by the word "unchastity" in the clause which provides an exception to the prohibition of divorce. The parallel passage in Mark 10:2-9 does not refer to an exception.

Chapter Five

The Story of The Fall Today

In Chapter Four we examined the meaning of Genesis 2-3 as intended by the *J* author as well as some of the meanings which were operative at the pre-*J* and post-*J* stages. As we now address the question of the meaning which this story can have for us today, it is important to remember the *multiplicity* of meanings which have come to the fore historically. Not only have we seen that the story and the earlier myths which lie behind it had different things to say to readers and hearers at different periods of history, but we have observed that even when speaking specifically of the meaning intended by the *J* author, the scholars who are supposed to be experts in these matters do not fully agree. At first this might seem discouraging to the reader who is not a scholar and had hoped for guidance from the experts. If, however, such readers are willing to accept the responsibility which comes as a consequence, then what at first seemed to be an unsettling state of affairs can become a liberating experience. The richness of a story such as that of the fall is precisely that it has many meanings. The role of the expert is not to pontificate about *the* meaning of the story, but to spark the creative process of interpretation, to open up possibilities by analyzing the material from a critical and historical perspective. This might establish certain broad boundaries beyond which interpretation cannot go without completely losing touch with the specificity of the story. However, within these boundaries there is room for a great deal of creativity, freedom, and originality. In the final analysis, each individual has the responsibility and the privilege of hearing the story and articulating "what this story means to me."

The conclusion of this book, therefore, is not going to present one modern interpretation which the reader is asked to accept. On the contrary, the readers are asked to relate the story to their own experience and to get into touch with what the story is trying to say to them. When the text is approached in this way, it will sometimes turn out that the contemporary reader will find that one of the *older* interpretations, such as those discussed in Chapter Four, continues to have meaning today. Such readers will reaffirm the meaning or meanings which past interpreters have found in the text. This way of going about the task of interpretation is so well known and so widely accepted that there is no need to discuss it at length. Instead, I would like to focus on more creative efforts to deal with the text, finding new meanings which we realize could not have been in the consciousness of the author and which do not have the sanction of ancient tradition. The willingness to depart from what the author meant, or what older interpreters said the story meant, may appear to be dangerously subjective. This process is indeed a subjective one, but that does not need to be a problem as long as we each take responsibility for our interpretations. If I am willing to "own" my interpretation and say "This is the meaning *I* find in the story," then I will not use it as an "authority" with which I try to compel others to agree with me, for the same freedom that I claim for myself must be allowed to others.

To illustrate what I am talking about, I will present two ways of interpreting Gen 2-3 in a contemporary context. It is hoped that what was said in the preceding paragraph will prepare the reader for the fact that both of these examples depart freely from the more historical type of interpretation which was done in Chapter Four.

First Example: "Judge Not and You Shall Not Be Judged." In this approach to Gen 2-3, we will be dealing with the process by which we judge persons, or their thoughts, feelings and actions, as being "good" or "bad." I am not referring to evaluations of objective matters such as the skills a person may have, but the kind of judgment which makes us want to separate ourselves from what is labeled "bad." This kind of judgment is most clearly identified by the emotions which go along with it. The "bad person" or that which is "bad" in a person triggers feelings such as anger, fear, anxiety, hostility, disgust, disdain, resentment and outright hatred.[1] It may be hard for us to recognize these feelings in ourselves because they are part of what we judge as "bad" and therefore try to hide. But if we are honest with ourselves, most of us will acknowledge that we do indeed make such judgments and have such feelings about persons. If we assume that the practice of judging in this way is not a necessary and inevitable part of life but is something about which we have a choice, then the concept provides a possibility for interpreting Gen 2-3. The decision to eat from the tree of knowledge of good and bad is understood as choosing to judge persons, including ourselves, as good or bad. Paradise, then, is the condition of peace and harmony which could be experienced if we chose not to judge. On the other hand, the condition of conflict, pain and alienation (real life?) described in Gen 3:14-19 as the punishment for Adam and Eve's disobedience is viewed as the result of choosing to judge.

It is possible to accept persons just as they are and to see them as beautiful and lovable without demanding that they change in order to gain our approval. This kind of acceptance or unconditional love is what we lose when we choose "to know good and bad," that is, to judge. We want to categorize persons, in whole or in part, as good or bad. Then we grant our love and approval according to these judgments. To do this we create criteria for evaluating people. These might be the criteria of a group to which we belong, or they might be our own private standards. We use them to judge whether persons are acceptable, adequate, O.K., or unacceptable, inadequate, not O.K. But there is a self-defeating outcome: when we judge others, we judge ourselves too. If other persons cannot be assumed to be acceptable and lovable just as they are, then neither can we! Therefore, when we think in this way, we are constantly evaluating ourselves, driving ourselves to live up to certain goals so that we will be able to accept and love ourselves. We think that we will be all right only if we lose a certain number of pounds, control our anger, become better housekeepers, get A's in school, get promoted at work, live in the right neighborhoods, or receive signs that certain people like us. We put ourselves under pressure to achieve standards which we have created or bought into. We are nagged by fear that we won't make the grade. When we fail to measure up, we experience guilt and shame. In order to convince ourselves that we are lovable and acceptable, we compare ourselves with others to see if we are closer to meeting the criteria than they are. Thus we experience ourselves as being in competition with others: if we can "put them down" we might feel better about ourselves. So one person acts as "master" over another, as Adam did after the fall (Gen 3:16). Furthermore, because we don't believe we are acceptable and lovable the way we are, we don't want other people to see us the way we are. So we cover ourselves and hide out of shame as Adam and Eve did with their fig leaves (Gen 3:7-10). Even worse, we pretend that we are something we are not in the hope of gaining acceptance from ourselves and others. We play phony roles which prevent genuine communication with others (cf. Gen 11:1-9), and eventually these masks fool even ourselves and we no longer remember who the real self is.

In summary, the choice to judge leads to pain and alienation. We are exhausted from striving to live up to criteria we have erected; we live in fear of failure; we experience shame and guilt when we do fail; we compete with others; we block honest communication and lose touch with who we are.

If such is the situation "after the fall," what would it be like if we gave up the habit of judging and undertook a return to paradise? This can be grasped experientially if the reader will try the following exercise. Sit comfortably and close your eyes. Take several slow deep breaths, allowing the exhalation to carry away any tension in your body and to quiet the busy activity of your mind. Visualize a beautiful garden with as much detail as possible. Become aware of the odors, hear the sounds, feel the air and the sun. Experience yourself as completely acceptable and lovable because you have just been created and must be exactly what God wants you to be. Savor the warmth of that acceptance and the joy which God has in looking upon you as a perfect expression of divine creativity. You realize that you do not need to pass any tests, measure up to any standards or put yourself under pressure to achieve. Your fellow creatures too are all perfectly lovable and acceptable as they are and they know that. You do not feel the need to judge them and they do not need to judge you. So there is nothing to fear, nothing to hide from one another. Each can be perfectly open because no one has anything to be ashamed of. Each one is free to be exactly what he or she was created to be, in cooperation rather than in competition. Each can work creatively toward growth and development in harmony with his or her own inner nature without any evaluations or comparisons. Peace, harmony, joy and creativity are experienced by all as their natural birthright.

If you try this exercise, using appropriate music in the background if you wish, you may become experientially convinced that the return to paradise is both desirable and possible.[2] In this way, the story of the fall emerges as a true story about us which helps us to understand the source of some of the pain in our lives and points to a way of living and thinking which leads to peace and joy. In New Testament terms, the injunction, "Judge not and you shall not be judged," is seen as a path leading to the kingdom of God.

Second Example: The Fall and Individuation. One of the essential processes in the growth and development of a human individual is the gradual separation from parents. This begins most visibly and dramatically at the moment of birth when the baby, which until then had been physically enclosed by the mother's womb, is suddenly expelled into the world. At this stage the child has become physically separate. According to psychologists who have studied the cognitive development of infants, however, the earliest sensory data received by the infant is interpreted in such a way that the baby understands the whole outside world as an extension of itself. It takes time before the infant differentiates between self and non-self. This too is a step of separation from the environment and of individualization. It does not take place on the physical plane, as birth did, but at the level of mind and thought.

Though the child is physically separate from the mother and understands it has an independent existence from the rest of the world, it is very much dependent upon parents and parent-surrogates for learning. The child's ideas of what is real and what isn't, its opinions on controversial issues, and the values on which it bases its behavior—all are learned from the parents. Even the child which appears to be willful and in conflict with the parents is acting on the basis of what has been learned from them. It is only as the final stages of growing up are reached that separation from the parental environment comes to completion at the level of knowledge and decision making.

Eating from the tree of knowledge of good and bad could be understood as the decision of the child to make up his or her own mind about what is true and to make his or her own decisions on questions of behavior. It is a stage in the growing process which can be painful for both the child and the parents.

All parents, of course, are eager for their children to become mature and "have a mind of her own" or "stand on his own two feet and make his own decisions." Nonetheless, it is often difficult for parents to give up the role which they have long had of shaping the thinking and decision making of their children. Although they want their children to reach this kind of adulthood, they might become anxious if the ideas and decisions reached in in this new stage of independence differ too radically from their own ideas and values. It is often the case that they will communicate at least some degree of pressure and disapproval.

The growing youngster, on the other hand, is likely to experience the growth process as one which is scary. The womb-like matrix of parentally guided ideas and decisions is being left behind as he or she becomes still more of an individual and more conscious of being separate and alone in the world. Even in the best of circumstances, the child is bound to feel some measure of guilt when his or her ideas and values differ from those imparted by the parents. When there is strong disapproval from the parents, this guilt might be quite severe. In addition, there might be frequent and intense conflicts with the parents which increase the feelings of fear, loneliness and separateness. The young person becomes aware of the responsibility to provide for his or her own needs "by the sweat of your brow." The fact that such experiences coincide with the coming of sexual maturity only adds to the turmoil.

The process of increasing individualization, beginning with physical birth, through early cognitive development, to independence in thinking and decision making, is, of course, completely natural. It is not "wrong" for it to happen. On the contrary, something would be terribly wrong if it *did not* take place. While the transition is not objectively sinful, however, it may well be experienced in such a way that it produces feelings of guilt and shame as the individual separates from the parental matrix. These feelings of guilt may leave long-lasting scars or even stunt the growth process. Seen in this context, the serpent of the story enters in as a helper who encourages the individual to believe that in spite of the real or imagined opposition of the parents, he or she cannot remain dependent but must dare to become "like gods" (i.e., like parents) making personal decisions about what is good and what is bad. This positive interpretation of the role of the serpent fits in with its reputation for being wise and having knowledge about life and healing. One finds this approach in psychological literature, especially by authors with a Jungian perspective. This departure from the usual Christian interpretation in which the serpent's advice leads to a sinful decision is not, however, completely absent from theological discussions of the Adam and Eve story.[3] A drawback of such an interpretation is that it views God too simply in analogy with the human parent. So while it provides helpful insight into the process of human growth, it is strictly limited in its depiction of our relationship with God.

Interpreted in connection with individuation, then, the story of the fall emerges as a (partially) true story about us which helps us to understand that conflict and pain must sometimes be accepted as inevitable concomitants of growth and that there is no going back to the womb of paradise. This interpretation must reverse the usual view (which was also the view of the *J*

author) that the choice which is made is a sinful one. This interpretation might be connected with another New Testament saying about the kingdom of God (Mt 10:34-35): "Do not suppose
that my mission on earth is to spread peace. My mission is to
spread, not peace, but division, I have come to set a man at odds
with his father. . . . "

Conclusion

The two examples of contemporary interpretation of Gen
2-3 sketched above have in common that they use the story as
symbolic of a contrast between two human states or conditions
and a kind of choice which presides over the transition from the
one state to the other. There are also interesting differences between the two interpretations. Some of these differences are
outlined in the following chart.

EXAMPLE ONE Judging	EXAMPLE TWO Individuation
The paradise state of not judg-ing is an ideal condition we can imagine though we have never been in it.	The paradise state of non-indi-viduation is the natural condi-tion into which we are born and through which we grow.
The states of paradise and the condition after the fall are ty-pological (not chronological) contrasts.	The state of paradise and the condition after the fall are chronologically sequential.
The state of paradise is more desirable than the condition after the fall.	The condition after the fall, in spite of the pain involved, is more desirable than staying in infantile dependency.
The choice to eat the fruit of the tree is a mistake which leads to loss.	The choice to eat the fruit of the tree is a necessary step in personal growth.

It is not possible to become any more god-like than we already are.	It is indeed possible to become "god-like" and that's what is involved in personal growth.
It is both possible and desirable to "return to paradise."	It is neither possible nor desirable to "return to paradise."

These two examples reflect a general model of how one might develop any number of specific interpretations of the story. The states before and after the fall can be taken to represent two conditions or ways of thinking and acting which are either chronologically sequential or typologically contrasted. The alternative corresponding to paradise may be viewed as either more desirable or less desirable than the condition after the fall. The choice involved in making the transition may be seen as a positive step, or as a mistake. Or all of these may be regarded as ambiguous, having advantages as well as drawbacks.

With all of these possibilities, there are many ways in which the story can be given contemporary interpretations which speak symbolically about important polarities and processes in our lives. Some of these interpretations will deal with what are essentially psychological issues, like the two examples I have presented. Others might find their inspiration in older views. For example, the polarity between obedience and disobedience might be seen as the crucial issue, precisely as was intended by the *J* author. Yet others may want to go further back into the history of interpretation and reaffirm the pre-*J* aspect of the story in which it was concerned with sexual maturity. As a further option, one might look to specific episodes in his or her own life history rather than to typical events which are universal in human experience. Finally, there may well be completely different ways of approaching the modern interpretation of this story—approaches which go beyond the general model which I am proposing. If so, all well and good, for my proposal is meant to stimulate creativity, not to stifle it. In any case, the symbol of movement into and out of the garden of paradise provides a rich paradigm which can help us clarify the way we understand ourselves.

At this point my task is ended and that of the reader begins. Inside me lurks a snake-like part which would tempt you to undertake the exciting experience of appropriating the story in your own way. Take a bite, if you dare, for the rest is up to you.

Notes

1. The more objective evaluations of skills mentioned above are not associated with such negative emtions. We may have a great love for Peter even though Paul is much better at fixing cars.

2. There are, in fact, a number of programs for personal growth which incorporate this principle and in which literally hundreds of thousands of people have embarked upon a path which has brought enrichment to their lives. See, for example, K. Keyes, *Handbook to Higher Consciousness*, 5th ed. (St. Mary, Ky: Living Love Publications, 1975) and G.G. Jampolsky, *Love Is Letting Go of Fear* (Toronto: Bantam Books, 1981).

3. See R.S. Hanson, *The Serpent Was Wiser: A New Look at Genesis 1-11* (Minneapolis: Augsburg, 1972).